The HOME

The HOME

EXCITING NEW DESIGNS FOR TODAY'S LIFESTYLES

Susan S. Szenasy

Macmillan Publishing Company
New York

Macmillan Publishing Company
866 Third Avenue
New York, New York 10022

Collier Macmillan Canada, Inc.

Library of Congress Cataloging in Publication Data

Szenasy, Susan S.
  The home: exciting new designs for today's lifestyles.

  Bibliography: p. 253
  Includes index.
  1. House furnishings. 2. Room layout (Dwellings).
3. Interior decoration—Amateurs' manuals. I. Title.

TX311.S96 1985   747.2'0498   85-4948

ISBN 0-02-600120-9

Macmillan books are available at special discounts for bulk
purchases for sales promotions, premiums, fund-raising,
or educational use. For details, contact:
Special Sales Director
Macmillan Publishing Company
866 Third Avenue
New York, New York 10022

10 9 8 7 6 5 4 3 2 1

THE HOME: Exciting New Designs for Today's Lifestyles
was prepared and produced by
Quarto Marketing Ltd.
15 West 26th Street
New York, New York 10010

Editorial Director: Marta Hallett
Art Director/Designer: Richard Boddy
Managing Editor: Naomi Black
Copy Editor: Pearl Hanig
Photo Research and Editing: Christine A. Pullo
Editorial Assistant: Louise Quayle

Typeset by BPE Graphics, Inc.
Color separations by Hong Kong Scanner Craft Company Ltd.
Printed and bound in Hong Kong by Leefung-Asco Printers Ltd.

For my sister, Judy Szenasy Toth, who has
made homes for her family on three continents.

CONTENTS

INTRODUCTION

Home design is the subject of a growing number of publications for the public at large. In the past, these have tended to fall into one of two major categories, defined as either the "how to" or the "wish" book.

The "how to" book is a holdover from the time when half the adult population was expected to find happiness in the home. These people needed, so the marketers of furnishings suggested, to be instructed in just how to "personalize" the mass-produced objects that were created by the other half.

The second approach, a more recent development, is the "wish," or "dreamer's," book. It assumes the availability of unlimited resources, the leisure time to spend them, and the peace of mind to enjoy the environment they can create.

In the eighties, however, the need for a third category of home design book is emerging. It is for those of us who find ourselves between the other two extremes. While we like to design and decorate some environments for ourselves, our time is too limited and our energies are too widely scattered to make the effort a major life focus. And then there never seems to be enough money to realize our inflated dreams. If we continue to think of our homes only as receptacles for the products we buy, both the "doing" and the "wishing" may become sources of frustration.

THE HOME is an attempt to satisfy the needs and demands of the third category of design-conscious homeowners. Its concerns are with making the available space fit the living and functioning needs of people. But space is next to impossible to describe. Its numerical measurements are deceptive. A house, for instance, may enclose 1500 square feet in such a way that every activity is accommodated gracefully. The same dimensions may cramp another household to the point of emotional exhaustion.

Thus, the organizing principle of THE HOME is space planning. Rather than discuss and prescribe a room-by-room, object-by-object treatment of the living space, THE HOME looks at the overall lifestyle of the individual or family, using this as a theme for interior space design. Therefore, the necessity and social function of consuming food is not necessarily relegated to the traditional spaces labeled "dining room" or "kitchen." Shown here are the multitude of ways that a utilitarian space design can be achieved for "eating," no matter where it takes place. This is a book that explores the questions that a design professional would ask of the new client: Who are we, how do we want to live, how do we actually live, and what does "home" really mean to us?

Visual literacy is a prerequisite to a rewarding achievement of space design. It implies something much more subtle than familiarity with popular styles. It is a result of living and looking and feeling. It is also the ability to find the words that bring back a memory of light and texture and color. THE HOME shows hundreds of examples of the variations on the theme of space design. Here are eating spaces that double as work areas, sleeping spaces that convert for entertaining, and passages that double for storing and displaying collectibles.

Before we can achieve a personal design that integrates visual literacy, we may need to talk about our physical experiences of coming home, walking through the house and arriving at various rest stops, eating, working, working out, bathing, and sleeping. These topics are explored in the general introductory text for each unit. With an array of examples, shown through pictures and captions, the specific alternatives, depending on desired lifestyle, are displayed.

How we approach each of these activities provides the clues to the amount of space we need for living and where each of these activities should be located. Thus begins the design process. And here is THE HOME to start us on our way.

Susan S. Szenasy

CHAPTER • ONE
ARRIVING HOME

The choice of where we live in the late-twentieth-century is determined by many factors, including the neighborhood's safety and negotiability by every member of the family, be they young or old; the building's energy efficiencies; its closeness to work, school, day care, shopping, and entertainment; and its ability to adapt as people change through time, because moving on and "trading up" to a more suitable home have become a speculator's paradise but a homeowner's financial nightmare.

Only a small fraction of housing is newly built, and often it is necessary to reuse and restore existing buildings as apartments and condominiums, or to tune up detached houses and the neighborhoods in which they stand. Both the home and its grounds, as well as their greater surroundings need to function for people whose needs have changed. The family group of the 1950s and 1960s that centered around the mother's unpaid labor is now a minority. Today the home also has to fit the complicated work and social lives of single parents and their children; couples each of whom considers career and home life important; and single persons, whose ages, incomes, and occupations run the gamut of the modern population profiles.

Although the computer promises to make the home an island of efficiency, it can also isolate us from one another. On the basis of social needs, many people are thinking of

The dormer window becomes a thoroughly new expression in a New England house. Each opening is designed as a unique light source for the room it serves.
Architecture: Graham Gund Assoc.
Photography: Steve Rosenthal

In Milan's historic center, nineteenth-century working-class buildings, with picturesque tiled roofs, wooden shutters, and balconies, are highly desirable places to live in the late twentieth century. While such courtyard buildings encourage neighborly interaction, they also require protection of individual privacy. The white, embroidered linen curtains serve this need as well as show that, here, the traditional crafts which made such buildings are still respected (see page 33).
Photo: Gabriele Basilico/Abitare

A modest budget of less than $50,000 stretched to build a gracious home for a young couple in Maine whose living space of 1,400 square feet on three floors is heated by a woodburning stove (see page 120). The house's birdlike charm derives from a symmetrically-warped pitched roof that follows the side walls' increasing height from front to back.
Design: Bentley/LaRosa/Salasky
Photography: Timothy Hursley

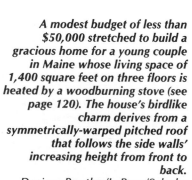

ways to reintegrate communities into human-scale groupings where neighbors work together to bring about occasions and services for the benefit of everyone.

The modern "village" is usually a developer's scheme of quaintly styled condos and detached houses, where the "community" swimming pool or golf course brings people together. Nearby support services are also required for families, so that parents don't have to drive extra miles to pick up children, food, and cleaning after they've extricated themselves from gridlocked traffic.

Motorways supplemented by paths, rest stops, commons, and play areas with benches expand the concept of home life to include the neighborhood. When coming home is a pleasurable experience, less time is needed to unwind, and more energy can be given to shared activities or to pursuing personal interests.

Whether we travel homeward to an urban maze, a suburban sprawl, or a rural scattering, we look for markers to tell us how close we are to the one place where we can safely unbuckle. When familiar landmarks—an evocative sculpture or fountain, a grove of willows, or a gable peeking through the foliage—greet us, the pleasure of coming upon their mysterious shadows, changing colors, refreshing scents and sounds lift the spirit.

Similarly, an attractive architectural detail that becomes a touchable familiar as we enter the front door welcomes us home. And when an object is designed with sensitivity to the light changes that time brings and with an understanding that a thing may be immensely satisfying both at a distance and close up, then a simple detail can be a source of many different experiences.

A neoclassical townhouse in a turn-of-the-century neighborhood has been filled with light for a young Chicago family who like to entertain their friends.
Architecture: Booth/Hansen & Assoc.
Photography: Paul Warchol

Even with the many and varied rooms to be inhabited in a Connecticut Victorian house, two twentieth-century necessities had to be added for comfortable living: the family room (see page 234) and the garage. The little house makes an easy connection between the two centuries, in function as well as in style.
Architecture: Shope Reno Wharton Associates
Photography: H. Durston Saylor

In Polo, Illinois, a corncrib is converted into a comfortable weekend retreat with the addition of windows, a deck, and a glass-enclosed room for the hot tub.
Architecture: Bauhs & Dring
Photography: Sadin/Schnair

A fanlight over the door may glow from the inside at dusk, dapple the interior hall on a Sunday morning, or filter the milky mist of midafternoon. Attention to small details like these make memorable homes out of houses. For even as the fanlight functions to make the hallway safe and bright, it adds unexpected dimensions to the experience of moving about. It's also a sign of human habitation and caring, akin to the impulse that built the fountain, preserved the willows, and lavished attention on the gables that have enriched our homecoming.

Because signs of personal expression are missing from most modern buildings, many people choose to restore and renew old, solidly built structures. Made with large windows—or the potential for these as well as for skylights, atria, and these clerestories, they have been built with lasting and attractive materials, embellished with details that show a belief in symbol and craftsmanship. Now they accommodate home living as cavernous interiors are divided up to fit the smaller-scale domestic life, displacing the large-scale industrial production of the past. The pattern has become familiar: Shortly after the evening news reports on the closing of a candy factory as hundreds of the newly unemployed file out toward an uncertain future, a newspaper story tells of the conversion into luxury condos.

As a result, today we live in watch factories, firehouses, stables, schools, churches, stores, grain silos, and corncribs. For the past decade these conversions have played havoc with one of the most often cited rules of design: Form follows function. It seems that function may not necessarily coincide with the intentions of a building's or product's designers. As successful adaptations of buildings tend to point out, a design is most meaningful and lasting when it accommodates possibilities far beyond its original intent.

In sections of cities where real estate values make renovation and restoration imperative, town houses are being turned back into the plush single-family homes for which they were designed at the turn of the century. Many choice pieces of Victorian architecture are also being converted to elegant small condominiums, in the process revealing the richly carved and polished woods, the ornamental plasterwork, the beveled glass, and the marble tiles that were once used to great advantage by the building trades, then were covered up by the detritus of nearly a century of living.

Mammoth apartment hotels—creatures of the turn of the century—created for the wealthy, who had minimal interest in housekeeping and enjoyed room service from the buildings' own restaurants, are making a comeback. Even as the old buildings, which had become rather frayed with age, are converted into the next crop of valuable cooperative apartments, a new generation of luxury highrise marketers sells condominium spaces the maintenance fees of which include hotel services geared to the wealthy professional couple, neither of whom wants to program the microwave.

Outside the central city, once a sea of single-family detached houses, the American landscape is changing noticeably. Now clusters of condominiums are being built to resemble giant châteaus, farm-houses, or haciendas, depending on a style's suitability to the climate and local building traditions. This trend of being "true to one's own region" is giving builders high marks for awareness mainly because their predecessors, dominated by the grid and encouraged by government policies of cheap energy, completely ignored local conditions. Indeed, the new clusters can save energy all around if the siting is able to capitalize on the special qualities of local sunshine, breezes, plantings, and materials in addition to being close to jobs, schools, services.

However energy-efficient cluster housing may be, like other forms of housing, it costs an immense amount of human energy to acquire and maintain. In the mid-1980s, an "incubator" condominium in California—a 340-square-foot box for

Stretching across the crest of a western Pennsylvania hill is a house made of many different buildings for an artist and a writer and their shared family life. From left to right, the separate buildings, connected by sheltered passageways, include the artist's studio separated from her small office house by a copse and a split rail fence along which she walks to the main house with its solarium, court-yard, and inner balconies (see page 34). This richly-towered assemblage of many different rooms includes the master bedroom in the Italianate turret; next to it the library under the apsidal roof; and the writer's cottage crowned by a cupola.
Architecture: Jefferson B. Riley of
Moore Grover Harper
Photography: Norman McGrath

In the Michigan dunes, in a thicket of local wild grasses and flowers cultivated by the resident who is an artist and an amateur naturalist, is an intensely private, decidedly manmade house that exists in great harmony with its environment. Approaching by a narrow, planked walkway, which first reveals the smaller of the two buildings that houses the artist's studio and the guest quarters, the visitor proceeds through a willow grove to the living quarters. Oriented against the southwest sun to protect the art collection, the house's long, windowless sides are made of steel panels, manufactured in the nearby Indiana steel towns. The short walls are all glass, giving each room a generous deck.
Architecture: Veronda Associates
Photography:© Bill Hedrich/ Hedrich-Blessing

On an untamed piece of land, surrounded on three sides by the waters of Long Island Sound, a small summer house (2,000 square feet) is a memorable addition for those who live here, their visitors, and the fascinated passers-by. It combines in an appealingly romantic way, nineteenth-century ideas about building that were developed along the northeast coast of the United States. Shingle, clapboard, and glass are variously used in the generous layering of rooms on three floors, the many different dormer windows, and the porches at all levels—including a widow's walk, which is accessible from a ship's ladder on the exterior. The sleeping porch, with its platform bed, suspends its occupants securely between sky and ocean, as other openings in other rooms create their own settings for summer dreaming (see page 220).
Architecture: Graham Gund Assoc.
Photography: Steven Rosenthal

Among the more flamboyant buildings of Coconut Grove, Florida, the house on Hibiscus Street is a landmark of understatement that combines local traditions learned from South American and German Bauhaus builders. The house's modified hacienda form, made of concrete block with a smooth stucco finish, protects the interiors from the tropical sun. The high windows of the living room, guarded by the loggia's tented canopy, help circulate the air. The upstairs bedrooms reach out to the open-air roofdecks. A hot tub is installed over the entrance tower that has a porthole.
Architecture: Andres Duany and Elizabeth Plater-Zyberk
Photography: Steven Brooke

The Saint Andrews Golf Community in Westchester, New York, was developed by golf pro Jack Nicklaus, who serves as chairman of the golf club and advisor to the restorers of the eighteen-hole golf course. Also restored on the property are the club house credited to the famous nineteenth-century society architect Stanford White, as well as Andrew Carnegie's former summer retreat, which has become a swim and racquet club for the new residents. The 209-unit luxury clusters comprised two- and three-level town houses, from 2,500 to 4,500 square feet of living space, are selling from $335,000 to $500,000 and up.
Architecture: Robert A. M. Stern
Photography: Edmund Stoecklein

South Florida's heritage of sheltering architecture is combined with the simple grids and cylinders of the International Style which, in its Mexican interpretation as practiced by Luis Barragán, has influenced the work of young architects in their use of color, monumental forms, and the surprises of their building plans. The pink ceremonial arch, which slices through a purple wall, pays a delightful homage to the mentor.
Architecture: Rodriguez Khuly Quiroga
Photography: Steven Brooke

Adjacent to an eight-lane freeway in San Diego, California, a small house (1,500 square feet), where the resident musician likes to hold concerts, is protected from its noisy environment by wrap-around stucco walls. Presenting a nearly blank face to the open road, with only one high window from an interior balcony opening in this direction, the house is centered on its courtyard and garden. A more generous view is celebrated by a balcony that juts out into the landscape.
Architecture: Rob Wellington Quigley
Photography: Tim Street-Porter

A Roman villa in Corpus Christi, Texas is a response to the extreme climates, which include annual hurricanes, as well as to the four-lane highway that passes nearby. The house, built of solid masonry, clad in Italian travertine, presents an introverted face to Ocean Drive, but opens itself up beyond the front door with an atrium to the sky; a colonnaded and trellised veranda facing the Gulf of Mexico; and a short "imperial" avenue that leads to the water.
Architecture: Batey and Mack
Photography: Tim Street-Porter

living—is being sold for $50,000 in the hopes, as one developer puts it, of getting people "in on the merry-go-round we call home ownership." In New York, the $500,000 "dockominium" is now the choice development scheme for hitherto-neglected waterfront properties.

Because we tend to view our homes as one more commodity, made to be used for a while, then replaced by another, we accept the available offerings with relatively little thought. The hard questions about how we want to live are often answered by decorative clutter. Or they may be answered not at all by ourselves but by market researchers and media advisers to builders, charged to attract buyers with romantic names for buildings and streets, embellished façades and lobbies, clever mechanical controls, and, now, celebrity tennis tournaments arranged to put the "fun" into searching for a home.

Increasingly, we search for other alternatives. In Maine, for instance, architects can build a house in the woods for the price of a California incubator. Weather-tight and solar-heated, such houses are thoughtful responses to concerns about nature and its resources and how people

want to live with both. In fact, many of the most interesting houses are built by architects who give their clients a sense of being in control of their immediate environments. There's genuine interest in making houses less technology-dependent. For those who live there, this can mean a life of added chores, like sowing morning glory seeds beneath the trellis that shades the south-facing windows, which will welcome the heat and light during the bare winter months but need to be protected from heat gain in the summer; maneuvering openings to catch the breezes, block the glare, and keep the heat from escaping; and stoking the woodburner to take the chill off.

What may appear to be merely a new interest in historical styles is often a serious study in making good houses. After decades of our ignoring the lessons of the past, it turns out that the Roman villa with its atria, grilles, colonnades, and solid masonry construction is a natural building type for warm climates. The nineteenth-century New England seaside house, with its many breeze-catching windows and small rooms piled on several floors, is perfectly adapted for the long summers of

childhood. Another nineteenth-century invention, the California balloon frame, can have an outside appearance of a constructivist metal sculpture with a homey inside, animated by its many different light sources.

There is, however, scant historical evidence on how to reconcile house, person, and car. Our main mode of transport lives inside the house as we do. It gets a big door, fitting its power, size, and importance. We—though powerful, large, and important in our imaginations— enter our section of the house through a small door that lands us in the kitchen, the family room, or, perhaps through some freakish twist of the floor plan, the spare bedroom.

The front door, like the erstwhile front parlor, seems to be an endangered species. But the acts of separating public and private behavior, the need to receive guests with some ceremony, the wish to welcome them to our special place demand that we continue the tradition of the front door. It's here that we begin to distinguish ourselves as people who are proud, intelligent, mysterious, artful, puritanical, practical, bland, or any other image we choose to adopt.

On a narrow (30- by-90 foot) urban lot in Venice, California two separate but connected houses have been built to take maximum advantage of light and views of the Pacific. The resident tower (see page 132) is attached to the rental building on one side by an open courtyard. The obliquely-angled structure has a balloon frame that allows the alternation of generous window and skylight surfaces with thick, insulating walls wrapped in a galvanized corrugated metal. Solar panels on the lower building heat the water for the house.
Architecture: Frank O. Gehry & Assoc.
Photography: Tim Street-Porter

The street's movement is slowed down and its scale is reduced by the walkway to the recessed front door.

In addition to the yellow-painted redwood siding and stucco, which were found on the original Los Angeles tract house, the tuned-up version adds another humble material, fiberglass shingles, which cover the attention-getting additions that were built to expand the living spaces of the main house and convert a former garage to a guest house and studio. Where the old house's former roof meets the new construction, a horizontal strip of wood becomes a memory; but more practically, in this earthquake-prone land, it stabilizes the structure. While the front door recedes into the house, the detail that indicates that something special is going on here is the roof, whose corners open up like the petals of a flower for a roofdeck and whirlpool (see page 198) that have views of the Santa Monica Freeway and the towers of Century City.
Architecture: Eric Owen Moss
Photography: Tim Street-Porter

Set inside an entrance niche which is lit from above by a skylight, the front door has a slight curve which reveals itself fully when the knob is turned.
Architecture: Eric Owen Moss
Photography: Tim Street-Porter

C H A P T E R • T W O

CIRCULATING

It is through movement that we get to know the world around us. If the house or apartment we live in allows us to move freely, without danger to life and limb, it has done half its job. It has accommodated the functions of living. But a home cannot be a mere accommodation. It should offer itself to us with generosity and good humor and appeal to our senses.

Movement needs to be considered more than mere locomotion. It can be a series of enriching moments. Added up, these form the story of our lives. The sight of a shaft of light after a rainfall changes the hallway from gloomy to hopeful. The muscular effort of ascending the stairs quickens our breaths. The touch of a railing accompanies our passage with safety. The sound of the wind promises a clear and bright day coming. And the scent of bread baking invites us to warm and nourish our bodies and souls in the company of others.

Home, then, is memories made by sensations, aspirations nurtured in security. Any design which shows an understanding of these has a rightness about it. We feel this instinctively, regardless of what styles are adopted. Such homes are lived in completely. Their entire area, inside and outside, is possessed by those in residence. The passages, then, are as important to the creation of a completely inhabited place as the rest stops to which they lead. Be they connectors between outside and inside or interior traffic directors, like doorways, halls, stairs, and landings, these spaces can expand in size and perception the usable areas for living. They can add, as well, many moments of pleasure to the ways we move about.

The front door addresses the issues which concern the whole house. The way we approach privacy, ceremony, and transition throughout begins to be communicated here. In addition, subtle or bold clues to who we are and who we aspire to be are given at the threshold.

As a point of transition the front door has a dual role to fulfill. It needs to remind the surrounding community of our unique existence (our public personas). At the same time it must separate us from that very same community (our private lives). This delicate balancing act of being part and apart from the world yields design opportunities of unusual richness, the importance of which we are only beginning to rediscover.

The front door can recede demurely into the building or hide itself completely from view. Its sheltering overhang provides a change in the exterior weather conditions while reducing the scale of the greater world to the size of the entering person. In cold climates, such entrances shield the inside from drafts; in the tropics they shade and promise a gradual cooling down as one moves through the interior.

The Front Door

Whether the house is one of many attached look-alikes or a unique structure that stands alone, its front can claim the space around it with great energy. Colors attract, as do textures. And when the two work together, the question of how design can integrate space and time is successfully answered: Colorful dots of plantings invite a closer look. Arrival can mean a rich juxtaposition of sights and scents. A lively mosaic of colors that flow together at a distance reveals always new details of special patterns at closer examination.

In each case the signs of human habitation are established. There's a person behind the door and beyond the pane who cared enough to trim the plants and display the artwork.

Lots of pink hanging plants add a seasonal greeting to the warm color of the front door, which is crowned by a delicate fanlight that brings in the sun year-round.
Photography: Jay Patrick/EWA

Nature invades, but not out of control, as the yellow front door asserts itself in the overgrown facade.
Photography: Ann Kelley/EWA

The same mosaic idea as that produced by fragments of materials is reduced to a flat paint treatment at the side entrance, distinguishing the hierarchical differences between the building's passageways.
Design: Dennis Jenkins
Photography: Steven Brooke

Pottery shards, tiles, and ceramic relief sculptures invigorate the walls around the door. The eye may catch an intricate pattern formation here or a texture there as it scans the surface from day to day.

CIRCULATING

The Entrance

The shape of the front entrance may promise the shape of things to come inside. The seemingly impassable front door with its oblique angle or thick barrier material may foretell a mysterious, reclusive interior. It can, as well, be a sheath that unfolds a series of surprises which confirm the generosity of the spirit within.

Although rooms may burst into one another or they may protect their secrecy, lively interior plans are given a secure feeling by the continuity of materials. The effect is especially pleasing when the small world within maintains a material kinship with the greater world without.

The rapid movement of the outside, be this a spicy urban stew of people and vehicles or a bland mechanization of suburban isolation, needs to be slowed to a more personal pace upon one's entering the house. For the body to feel the difference between the two environments, it should arrive in a place which is cushioned from the outside breezes and noises.

While the urban arrival is likely to be a small niche devised by clever anglings of walls and doors, the suburban point of transition may be a generous space of sun, vegetation, and other materials that bring in the elements from the surrounding landscape.

The arched front door with its simple carved detailing opens to a foyer of this French house, where the inviting curve is repeated in the interior window. The choice of the cabinet continues the aesthetic harmony of shapes.
Photography: Robert Harding
Picture Library

The volcanic stones which pave the street are cut into tiles to form the stairs that amble through the entryways of this Mexican house. The bougainvillaea's color is imitated on the outside and continued on the inside.
Architecture: Luis Barragán
Photography: Allen Carter

An angled partial wall with a windowed door creates a small entrance hall in a modest Milanese apartment. It helps avoid an abrupt arrival into the main rooms, to which the front door originally opened when the house was built in the nineteenth century. The lovely lace-trimmed curtains and the curves of the furniture recall design history.
Architecture: Yolanda Collamanti Wiskemann
Photography: Gabriele Basilico/ Abitare

Not only the sun but the things that it energizes are brought into a space that lights and warms itself and the surrounding rooms. The rough brick floor and the ivy-covered walls have all the charm of an outdoor terrace, but this one can be used year-round.
Design: Mr. and Mrs. Janssens
Photography: Karen Bussolini

Niched into the façade of the building (see page 16), surrounded by balconies on each side, and roofed over with glass, this solarium-entrance hall openly reveals the public rooms of a house built for a Pennsylvania writer, sculptor, and their child.

CIRCULATING

The Central Hall

The central hall, which gathers arrivals and disperses them throughout the house, is being reconsidered as architecture becomes infused with a new richness of expression. Such formal solutions have a tendency to organize movement around vanishing-point perspectives. The symmetries which gather around these give strong directional indicators.

The use of a greenhouse as an entryway is significant beyond the romantic wish to live in harmony with nature. It is a practical solution which helps heat the house during the cold months. When the south-facing solarium entrance hall is backed by a wall of concrete blocks—a material which absorbs the heat of the sun—the building helps heat itself by its own natural radiation. Thus, the wall which holds up the structure and separates the several functions of the house becomes a radiant heating source which helps decrease reliance on mechanical solutions.

High, vast spaces surrounded by open balconies become places where the eyes register the generous overhead canopy and the many possibilities for movement which are offered. Such spaces also allow free circulation of air and light, which give freshness and immediacy.

Like the courtyard of a building, the open interior balconies provide opportunities for exchanges between household members whose private lives and occupations are well protected by the many passages and doors throughout the house.

The central hall's sun-absorbing concrete wall is plastered with gray cement and etched with shadowy images by the artist who lives here and the architect who designed the house. The passage to higher ground is marked by a collection of exquisite ceramic pieces, placed in stepped-up niches decorated with contrasting green paints and lighted from a window on the end wall.

The living area, separated from the front hall by the overhead balcony and the oriental rug which centers to the fireplace, is a cozy retreat of traditional forms and materials in the midst of great openness and freedom of movement. The balcony fronts an upstairs bedroom and is used as a sitting area.
Architect: Jefferson B. Riley of Moore Grover Harper
Photography: Norman McGrath

CIRCULATING

The Doorway

The openings to rooms are often unremarkable functional funnels which promise "efficient" circulation throughout. Doors are often missing, as are other divisions between rooms.

Yet a new interest both in decorative detail and in creating houses that are truly lived in has focused attention on separating rooms and on designing special doorways for them. Size and ornament once again are considered physical indicators of the expectations of behavior beyond the door.

A narrow, thick-walled entry to a room can provide a moment of surprise as one passes from its confines to the larger open space. A generous, formal doorway indicates a sense of decorum.

The Edwardian character of this London flat has been reinforced by the tall ceremonial connection between the rooms designed for living and dining, decorated by the simple molding and the characteristic cream-colored paint.
Architecture: Jon Wealleans
Photography: Richard Bryant

The new love of decorative detail in the late twentieth century comes to a New York apartment by way of a generously sized arched doorway which integrates high-tech steel with the postmodern colors of pink and slate.
Architecture: Leslie Armstrong
Photography: Norman McGrath

Because the old architectural stonework around two different doorways in an Italian farmhouse has been uncovered, the act of entering has been given two different feelings: one ceremonial, one less so. The strip of rust-colored paint at the wall's base continues the brick color of the floor and reinforces the step to higher ground.
Design: Teresa Pomodoro and Giancarlo Montebello
Photography: Antonia Mulas/ Abitare

CIRCULATING
The Door

The simplest and most convincing architectural tool for expressing the need to be alone or the wish to be part of the group is the door. It keeps out the cat, filters cooking odors, muffles electronic bits and bytes, and then lets all these rush in when the mood is more receptive to the rich life of the household.

But the door is much more than an element of control. It is capable of expressing its functions as a traditional barrier that pushes open and pulls shut on its hinges; it can slide out of its site or fold up into a compact decorative detail; it can pivot and behave like a piece of abstract sculpture that provides teasing views into the space beyond.

The light from the generous windows moves freely between the living room and guest bedroom of a renovated Milan apartment when the sliding door is left open.
Architecture: Yolanda Collamanti Wiskemann
Photography: Gabriele Basilico/ Abitare

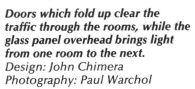

Doors which fold up clear the traffic through the rooms, while the glass panel overhead brings light from one room to the next.
Design: John Chimera
Photography: Paul Warchol

The door between the open living area and the more secluded bedroom can pivot shut as the high panels on hinges close for complete privacy in the night zone.
Architecture: Steven Holl
Photography: Paul Warchol

The symmetrical positioning of columns and the strong ceiling grid both separate and unite the open room's different areas.
Architecture: Batey and Mack
Photography: Tim Street-Porter

CIRCULATING

The Open Plan

For the most part of this century the open plan interior has been explored as an alternative to many small rooms divided by walls and doors. Superstrong slim-profile materials have all but eliminated the need for interior supports, clearing the way for an unprecedented freedom of movement for people, light, and air throughout the house.

Such universal spaces can be made more personally inhabitable by strongly defined ceiling grids or beams, low floor levels alternating with higher grounds and a predictable progression of columns. A curved wall which may reach the ceiling or stop short of it, changes in the color and texture of materials are some of the successful devices that give the rules for movement through an open interior.

A curved wall shelters the dining room on one side and hides the open bedroom on the other. The change in floor covering from hard to soft and the position of the brightly painted steel column with its uplights mark the transition from public to private areas in the New York apartment.
Design: Ward Bennett
Photography: Norman McGrath

CIRCULATING
The Corridor

The hallway is a prolonged entrance to a room. As such, it can cool tempers or fire imaginations during the time that it takes to funnel energies from one area to the next. But more than a mere conduit, a corridor is increasingly pressed into active duty as the household goes about finding ways to accommodate the proliferating paraphernalia of living. Collectons of books, wines, or art, clothing or toys, dinnerware or sports equipment, require constant maintenance and easy retrieval. The signs of these activities closely integrate passageways with their surroundings, infusing the whole house with the sparks of living.

When hallways are truly inhabited, they provide occasions for delight and mystery, in addition to being utilitarian containers. A glance at a colorful painting on the end wall can give a flash of pure aesthetic pleasure or a moment of proud ownership. Light coming from an unseen source can arouse one's curiosity or lure another to a favorite spot. So the function of getting from here to there becomes a rich experience of activities, feelings, and expectations.

Hallways leading to private areas of the house can provide occasion for public displays. This one, lined with mirror on one side and open shelving for Central American art treasures on the other, leads to a bathroom.
Design: The Space Design Group
Photography: Mark Ross

Author Geoffrey Archer's living room is entered through his well-stocked library, which is located in the corridor. The arch of the ceiling is a friendly gesture to arrivals.
Photography: Morley von Sternberg

Light and texture are given to this hallway by a long, narrow niche which contains a collection of statuary, paintings, and glassware. The Gothic woodwork emphasizes their importance.
Design: Jean and Martin Corke
Photography: Michael Dunne/EWA

A wine collection, part of it located inside the temperature-controlled cabinet behind the glass door, part of it stored at room temperature in honeycomb shelving, is a sparkling addition to a small hall.
Design: Sharon Pretto
Photography: Bill Rothschild

The lively red-and-white paint which gives a welcoming glow to a much-used hallway provides a decorative background for the many things that may be stored in open shelving and closet spaces.
Design: Nelson Demmy Designers and Builders
Photography: Karen Bussolini

CIRCULATING
The Stairway

The stairway is a potent architectural expression of the moving body. It requires noticeable muscular exertion imposed by the pull of gravity. Because of this, the effort needed "to scale the heights" may turn stairs into frustrating physical and mental obstacles for some, even as others find them exhilarating challenges.

Architects, talking about the stairs they build, often sound like choreographers as they describe the direction, rhythm, and pacing involved in their designs. Because these things are subject to broad interpretations, a stairway is a unique support not only for walking but for surveying the interior and exterior surroundings from constantly changing points of view.

An oblique and slowly rising path, for instance, lets the body meander through space, allowing the eyes to take in the scenery even as the body slips through gentle level changes. Quite different is the experience of a twisting or precipitous rise, which presents an element of danger and requires careful attention to the act of moving and holding on. A mixed pacing of steep steps with generous landings, on the other hand, can speed up and slow down movement simultaneously.

A barely noticeable incline meanders through a water lily pond that connects parts of the house. The elongated steps add to the enjoyment of the leisurely pace required in a Balinese garden.
Architecture: Henk Vos
Photography: Tim Street-Porter

That the activity of ambulating is enriched by its setting has been well known to builders through the ages. Small niches with decorative possibilities punctuate a turn where the steps change direction in a spiraling motion.
Photography: Michael Dunne/EWA

A shaft of light shooting through several layers of space is traveled by a spiral stair. Every turn brings a new visual delight. Safe passage is assured by the railing.
Design: Jack Lenor Larsen
Photography: Paul Warchol

For the daring, it's a walk-up to the roof; for the less nimble, the ladder becomes a coat or hat rack.
Design: Chester Jones
Photography: Michael Nicholson/ EWA

A steep stairway, looking like a relief sculpture that decorates the tall living area, leads to the open rooms of the mezzanine.
Architecutre: Stanley Tigerman and Margaret McCurry
Photography: Karant + Associates

The golden glow of the painting on the landing wall, lit from above, draws the eye and body toward it while the dramatic pink- and gray-painted wall and stair give an abstract sculptural quality to the simple passage through time and space.
Architecture: Luis Barragán
Photography: Allen Carter

Leisurely progress, encouraged by the boldly colored, elongated steps which jut sculpturelike into the sunlit living room, changes to a brisk walk up the stairs, which are concealed by a paneled partial wall that lets light and air travel between upstairs and downstairs. A small door, which opens to storage under the stairs, is concealed by the grooves of the paneling, which also lines the thick doorway that leads to the dining room.
Architecture: Yolanda Collamanti Wiskemann
Photography: Gabriele Basilico/Abitare

Vertical movement through Lord Carrington's house is an adventure in light, texture, and art. Ledges are used for displaying objects, and so are the walls, which become densely packed surfaces that require attention and give back countless moments of amusements.
Photography: Morley von Sternberg

Wasted space under a stairway is claimed for a wine collection which makes a decorative virtue of bottles and racks.
Photography: Frank Herholdt/EWA

The muscular tension built into steeply rising stairs is relieved by a cushioned bench which backs into the landing and doubles as a railing. Marking the moment of arrival is the spherical detailing of the railing, which visually slows down the insistent pattern created by thin slats.
Architecture: Graham Gund Assoc.
Photography: Steve Rosenthal

CIRCULATING
The Landing

Landings can become little rooms where movement is suspended and tense muscles relax for a moment before locomotion resumes. The most considerate of these in-between spaces offer a chair, a bench, a ledge where it's possible to sit for a moment and assess where one has come from and where one is going. And when the eyes can wander for a moment to the outdoors or through the expansive and varied interiors, the rest stop becomes a moment that refreshes both mind and body. Tables and shelves with a thoughtfully placed telephone or a mirror are equally useful to visitors and to members of the household.

When the sliding door to the game room is pocketed inside the wall, light from four directions fills the landing. Even when the door is shut, wide vistas of nature and the interior world below offer themselves for contemplation.
Architecture: Gwathmey Siegel
Photography: Norman McGrath

A selection of decoy ducks and other handmade objects, placed on a richly carved antique table, basks in the sunny niche at the top of an old house's stairs.
Photography: Michael Dunne/EWA

A private moment on the telephone is supported by a comfortable chair and a cantilevered console which stores pencils and notepaper. The conversation is made memorable by the delightful cocks in mock combat, painted by "Chucho" Reyes.
Architecture: Luis Barragán
Photography: Allen Carter

The link between the main house and the new family room is traversed under a lavender-painted tympanum ceiling with its contrasting cornice, which introduces the small dot pattern that is repeated in the areas that follow.

CIRCULATING
The Detail

Wood and paint, two traditional tools of domestic architecture, are used with a new freedom to celebrate the everyday acts of moving about by adding special details to the interior. A new generation of architects, much like their influential mentors, Frank Lloyd Wright and Le Corbusier, study the nature of their materials and feel at ease with designing ornament, which they, as craftsmen themselves, can interpret with authority to their tradesmen. The balustrade, the handrail, and the post become organic expressions of the total design, not merely applied decoration, which can be overly precious and eclectic.

The stairway provides an opportunity to think about three-dimensional design. It may be a place to hide small visual surprises learned from Michaelangelo's grand staircase in the Laurentian Library, with its perversion of scale that exaggerates height and depth and playful use of supporting elements. Such "tricks" delight residents and may mystify visitors.

A taller than expected post directs traffic to the upper floors, accompanied by the lively pattern of uprights. The fine detailing of the post's shaft and crown also marks the arrival at the landing halfway up the stairs.

From the balcony—with its finely-detailed, painted balustrade—a person may survey the traffic under the skylight, the shaft of which has been adopted as the favorite passage by the members of the household.
Architecture: Shope Reno
Wharton Associates
Photography: H. Durston Saylor

The area of Eastern Europe is a largely unexplored territory of unique crafts which were practiced for generations, then lost their vitality in the drive toward global mechanization. One small nation may have dozens of regional decorative styles, and the differences from country to country are dramatic. Simple floral bouquets and borders decorate traditional Polish stoves, dishes, and fabrics.
Photography: Robert Harding Picture Library

C H A P T E R • T H R E E

SHOWING OFF

DECORATION, ORNAMENTATION, AND COLLECTIONS

"...what is any art but an effort to make a sheath, a mould in which to imprison for a moment the shining, elusive element which is life itself," wrote Willa Cather in *The Song of the Lark*. Paying no heed to hierarchies which would make craft into the poor relation of high art, she went on to admire paintings, Indian pottery, and operatic performances frankly because they "made one feel that one ought to do one's best."

Once we were all artists. We saw the flowers and painted or carved them on our walls and furnishings, embroidered them on our fabrics, and burned them into our serving vessels. Nobody bothered to separate the use of an object from its beauty, its shape from its ornament. It was all one piece. It showed that someone cared to spend the time, give the thought, and do the work which happened to add a moment of pleasure to something that would also be useful if no such effort had been made.

Then ornament became crime, the artist became a producer, the paycheck became the reward, and art became something separate from life, a rare item to be displayed in museums or purchased by connoisseurs. The rest of us were left to feel ill at ease with objects we couldn't understand unless a scholar explained them to us.

The progressive abstraction of art and architecture—though often talked about as a play of simple forms made for universal comprehension—produced a yearning for expressions which would infuse the hard-edged product of the intellect with the softness of emotions.

The movement to restore, revive, and reuse is a comment on some of these vague yearnings. It signifies a realization that generations before us, in cultures often alien to ours, made things that touch us, that capture our imaginations, and help us become more thoughtful occupants of our time and place in history.

↑

Buildings that give back to their environments what they freely offer become unforgettable places to be. So our memories return again and again to the Mexican stables which repeat in their simple geometric shapes the lush, bright local colors, the monumental architecture of the past, the strong light and shadow play of the region, and the reflections and sounds of life-giving waters.
Architecture: Luis Barragán
Photography: Allen Carter

DECORATION
The Garden

Stylistic trends come and go. At varying times we pledge allegiance to the simplicity that was the Parthenon; then the fantasy of Disneyland grabs hold of our imaginations and shows up in all sorts of objects, from clocks to carpets. Through it all, nature remains the superstar of decorators. Although much modern thinking appears to have forgotten that we are its creatures, the world around us protests our neglectful ways as the air becomes too thick and the water runs in a strange yellow stream from the tap.

Some say that our constant and often nostalgic search for home—that elusively romantic place where we long to belong—is a symptom of our loss of contact with nature. This is confirmed when we search our memories about the places where we have felt truly at home. These might reveal a remembrance of the afternoon sunlight as it warmed the yellow pine floor, or the delicate movement of

gauze curtains in the breeze, or the sound of water flowing into a stone fountain accompanied by birdsong.

Earth and its colors and textures, water and its sounds and reflections, animated by the two other elements—fire and its light, air and its movement—teach us about form and ornament. Frank Lloyd Wright, the most influential architect of modern times, knew this, and he never tired talking about the lilies of the field and their decorative beauty, which is inseparable from their form.

Nature continues to inspire decorators. Each season, new fabric and wallpaper

Decoration that lives, moves, and appears again and again fills the house and its gardens with an infinity of visual surprises. A colorful bird lands on a branch; flowers drop into a small stone pool; statues get dressed up for a party. These details, like the open house which they inhabit, give texture to the richly varied experience of life in Bali.
Architecture: Henk Vos
Photography: Tim Street-Porter

collections promise to refresh tired rooms with lively botanical patterns straight from hothouses, be these real or imaginary. The chintz-covered sofa and its color-coordinated chair companions, the lushly draped window, and the freshly ornamented walls which surround it bring us back, again and again, to the pages of decorating magazines in search of the fantasy garden that might be our home.

Equally compelling are the decorative surfaces which require more than the services of the upholsterer and the paperhanger. Murals and various other wall paintings challenge artists who like to explore the depth and dimension which may be given to flat surfaces much larger than the easel can hold.

South Florida decorates itself with a profusion of luscious flowers. An edited version of these appears poolside, gathered in ceramic pottery.
Architecture: Barry Sugarman and E. D. Stone, Jr.
Photography: Steven Brooke

Traditional Japanese houses, with their empty interiors, which convert to accommodate many situations as the simple paraphernalia of living is brought out from storage, are integral with nature. The subdued textures and colors of the interior are mere backdrops to the profusions of decorative schemes provided by the ever-changing surroundings.
Photography: Robert Harding Picture Library

One of the most abiding dreams is the romantic wish to dine in a garden. A mural, painted to resemble a gazebo, is a perpetual day in the country, minus the flies diving into the cherry pie. The large parasol overhead continues the sheltering enclosure depicted by the surrounding painting on walls and window shutters.
Design: Jane Fry
Photography: Christine Hanscomb
© Condé Nast

No longer useful as a work tool, an old winepress becomes a potent reminder of people and their occupations before our time, even as the gathering of plants promise the continuation of the life cycle.
Photography: Robert Harding Picture Library

DECORATION

The Stencil

Perhaps because the marketplace is flooded with a wealth of manufactured decoration which is rotor- or flatbed-printed and stamped onto any imaginable surface, there's a strong tendency to seek out the unique, the one of a kind. In such a climate, old crafts are revived, their uses assessed, and their decorative possibilities extended.

Stenciling, a method of applying decoration by painting through cutouts in

Simple rustic furniture is in perfect harmony with the delicate stencil designs of potted geraniums which alternate with a trellis pattern and a tall fountain in a painted niche. The realistic shading of the stenciled images fools the eye, as the real and the fake plants are placed side by side to create together the garden-fresh decoration of the room.

Sanded and bleached floors stenciled with a stylized fruit basket pattern coordinate with a border design adapted for the tablecloth. Other fabrics on windows and on the bed continue the wreath pattern which appears on the walls.
Design: Lyn LeGrice
Photography: David Cripps/EWA

heavy paper or metal is once again used by architects. They study the decorative arts of the late-nineteenth century and recognize the rich traditions that were left behind when a worldwide search for a machine-age aesthetic began to take hold in the 1920s.

As the work of people like William Morris, Louis Comfort Tiffany, and Louis Sullivan is studied, their talents as virtuoso patternmakers, whose exotic, demandingly intricate designs challenged the best Victorian stencil cutters, are admired and emulated.

Now with fast-drying paints and clear polyurethane coatings that seal floor finishes, stenciling is considered an attractive alternative to other floor patterns. In addition to its traditional use on walls, ceilings, furniture, and fabrics, stenciling is an appealing addition to other surfaces.

An example of the international Art Nouveau style was found in Philadelphia by two architects whose theoretical writings and buildings helped create a new interest in ornament and decoration. Denise Scott Brown and Robert Venturi restored the 1910 building and added their own, highly inventive system of stenciling. In the dining room the walls are patterned with designs which combine the early styles with the fragmented look of today. The stenciled frieze is a sinewy stalk which ties together a decorative cornice pattern made by names of artists admired by the couple.
Architecture: Denise Scott Brown and Robert Venturi
Photography: Paul Warchol

A sinewy design, today's interpretation of a fashionable style which was the rage among the trendy and chic when the nineteenth century fused into the twentieth, is stenciled on the wall behind a small Art Nouveau cabinet. The delicate but assertive wall painting calls attention to the highly decorative piece of furniture inspired by plant life. This short-lived style, which had its own regional expressions from Scotland to Finland to Hungary and beyond, was characterized by tendrillike curves, inlays of stained glass and mother-of-pearl, and richly polished woods from which the cellulose fairly screams.
Architecture: Jon Wealleans
Photography: Richard Bryant

DECORATION
The Photo

Faking it is fun. Or that's what the current expressions, labeled collectively trompe l'oeil, or fooling the eye, seem to say. A wall may become a Chinese garden; a floor may resemble the exquisite marble inlays of a Russian czar's winter palace; a ceiling may open onto a sunny sky patterned with hovering clouds.

All these are painted, often with the intention of giving depth through perspective, pattern, and color to flat surfaces in small and potentially confining apartments. These blank stages of modern living seem to cry out for the newly liberated flights of artistic fancies.

Where a painter is not available, there's a growing selection of products which can imitate the imitations. Wallpapers today— as they did in that other decorating boom of a century ago—come in large choices of scenic designs, can add "architectural detail" with patterns designed to look like coffered ceilings, fancy cornices, and dadoes, resemble the graining of rich materials from marble to lapis lazuli. The decorative thought may be carried even further by the use of fabrics which resemble the wallpapers which recall the paintings which imitate the real thing.

The invention of photography has added its own voice to this clamoring for ornament. The camera has a unique ability to zoom in, to highlight a small or

The dining room is simply a stone-top garden table and two tall and thin standing lamps. This spare room, like the others, is decorated by the photographic images of a Renaissance building detail. The overhead bookshelves, underscored by a lettered legend, which surround the room like an old-fashioned cornice, become a modern space extender.

previously unnoticed decoration and bring it into view. Close-ups of beautiful building details bring history in close contact with people.

The forms and aesthetic concerns of the Renaissance, for instance, may be brought to light and integrated into modern life. A blowup of an architectural shell detail, found in one of the paintings of Piero della Francesca, is repeated many times to make a wall covering for a small apartment in Milan.

In addition to providing a highly decorative surface, the photographs are rich with other meanings. They remind the residents of the innovative work that preceded them, which occupied one fifteenth-century artist who became known for his masterful use of perspective and his unique ability to use light to create an atmosphere.

In the bedroom the narrow space dictated the lining up of two divans foot to foot, in a niche created by the double bookshelves. The photographic images extend to the ceiling and disguise the closet door.
Architecture: Mariella Frateili
Photography: Gabriele Basilico/
Abitare

DECORATION

Fragments

Fragments, those bits and pieces of memory which we allow to float to the surfaces of our consciousness, find material expressions in architecture and design. No longer asked by the ruling taste to banish the thought, design professionals are producing houses and furnishings which brim with rich references to historical styles. As a result, excerpts dating from as far back as the Egyptian pyramid to as recent as the 1950s tract house are being applied with little inhibition about what is "correct."

We may, then, truly be coming to the time when "the essential you," that elusive personality which has been stalked by decorating magazines since the invention of the medium, is about to surface and show itself as an idiosyncratic creature of complexities and contradictions.

This brave new world of decorating freedom can tolerate widely different approaches. One person may invest a great deal of scholarly research into restoring and highlighting ornamental plasterwork. Another may simply peel away layers of accumulated plaster and paint and decide that the resulting surface is a highly decorative expression of the history of the house.

Existing ornamental plasterwork, woodwork, and moldings are highlighted by paint, reinforcing the room's traditions, even as the mottled walls give it an up-to-date texture. With views of London's Stanley Crescent, the room, like its surrounding cityscape, maintains an easy relationship between past and present.
Design: Peter Farlow
Photography: Christine Hanscomb

Metallic flecks make the walls shimmer in the light and add a modish touch to the traditional design of the small but tall London flat. A band of scalloped fleur-de-lis below the ceiling ties the eclectic furnishings together with a decisively decorative touch.
Design: David Fielding
Photography: Christine Hanscomb

A wild streak of mosaic runs up a rough-plastered wall which has been splashed with the hot colors of the tropics. The pottery shards recall the more detailed mosaic of the front entrance (see page 29).

When renovation work on a South Florida house revealed rich layering of colors and textures, these were left in their natural state and became an unorthodox wall decoration that takes literally the current wish to uncover historical detail.

Referring to the more deeply textured mosaic design, a flat painted surface also harkens back— in its amorphous shape—to the peeled-away paint and plaster of the interior wall, each a fragment of imagination that relates easily with another fragment.
Design: Dennis Jenkins
Photography: Steven Brooke

Although the modern idea of openness is served admirably, the walls give a strong definition to each room. They aid interaction between the separate areas by the transparency and translucency designed into their forms. The green wall stands like an abstract sculpture between the dining room and the living room beyond. It presents fragments of one room to another while the Magritte painting comments on a more fantastic environment. The glass block wall shimmers in its own light while shedding the light over the adjacent spaces.
Architecture: Gwathmey Siegel
Photography: Norman McGrath

ORNAMENTATION
The Wall

Just as ornament may be applied to a surface, it may, as well, be inseparable from a structure. A wall, that traditional divider of human functions, may be designed as a piece of sculpture. Its materials are the time-tested materials of contemporary architecture.

With its smoothly curving edges, its cutouts, which decorate one space with selective views of another, and its surface painted in an attractive color, such a wall is rich in ornament, although it is clearly undecorated.

A wall made of glass becomes a living reflection of the people and objects around it, playing in patterns and textures which change from moment to moment. Glass block, for instance, now comes in a large selection of patterns, from starbursts to grids to ripples, in several sizes and shapes. The walls made from these filter and facet light into many decorative fragments. Originally, glass block was used in industrial buildings. Now, it has a new life in interior decoration.

In this atmosphere of change and cross-fertilization of ideas, other types of glass, with even longer histories and more colorful pasts, are finding new applications in architecture. The most decorative of these, stained glass, is an art form which is now practiced with great energy and creativity. It has brought a new richness of design, pattern, color, and detail into the house. So have etched and beveled, opaque and translucent glass surfaces; all working to expand our decorative options to ornament while celebrating light.

Layers of glass—each a different quality—work toward total translucency and material richness. The curtain wall of the modern Chicago high-rise, the curved glass walls ornamented by a transparent aluminum-mesh wave pattern which define the dining room, and the interior glass block walls combine into a sculpture for living. Here the traditional building materials of modern architecture—glass and steel—constantly changed by light, allow no distinction between art and life.
*Architecture: Krueck and Olsen
Photography: © Bill Hedrich/
Hedrich-Blessing*

*In an entrance hall a wall of light and color has been created in stained glass. Its bold design and intriguing textures update a traditional art form, making it an appropriate ally of modern architecture.
Design: Ken van Roenn
Photography: Robert Perron*

ORNAMENTATION
The Ceiling

Structural elements have been sources of satisfying ornament since wooden beams, left unfinished, called attention to the play of light and shadow overhead. With the modern addition of highly tensile steel supports, which are often hidden under plain surfaces, construction became occupied with expanding the freedom of movement through open spaces.

Attention is called to the ornamental possibilities of metal structural elements. Thin and elegant, the ceiling's beams and planes are highlighted by color and texture, as is the floating staircase, which is at once a striking sculpture and a conveyor of vertical movement in the open space. The crisp striped awnings protect the interior from glaring light. The venetian blinds disappear into a thin line of metal when complete transparency between interior and exterior is desired.
Architecture: David Hovey
Photography: © Bill Hedrich/
Hedrich-Blessing

The resulting interiors—architects like to call them universal spaces—are indeed capable of adapting to the various needs for privacy which one is likely to require during a long lifetime. Simply by the addition or removal of partial or full walls—without fear of the roof's collapsing—the home has become a flexible place where space can be pushed into new shapes and sizes, segmented as the times of our lives require.

While the virtues of freedom of movement—be it of persons or light and air—were the main occupation of architects, their tendency was to ignore ornament altogether or to make it so refined that the untrained eye had trouble locating it.

Then it was discovered that industry-produced structural elements had a great deal of decorative appeal of their own. Exposing the ceiling plane, with all its conduits, beams, wires, and pipes, could add an abstract relief sculpture overhead, whether it was highlighted with paint or left in its "natural" state.

The systems from which ducts and track lights are suspended, long familiar to those who work in airplane hangars, found their way into the home, as did the open steel beams of factory ceilings, now fashionably highlighted by bright colors

The metal ceiling grid becomes a delicate mesh of ornamental pattern while it serves to support track lights and suspends the air-conditioning ducts, which have an attractive "natural" texture of their own. Underscoring the metal module established overhead is the subtle ornament in the floorboards made by strips of teak wood. These are used to connect visually yet to divide the living and dining areas, which are, in fact, separated only by the partial wall of the fireplace.
Architecture: Veronda Associates
Photography: © Bill Hedrich/
Hedrich-Blessing

The simple paneling of the ceiling and of the partial walls are given a special decorative accent with paint. The ceiling's mustard-colored design duplicates the actual shape of the room, which has been created by the installation of the partitions, while it adds a lively decoration.
Architect: Yolanda Collamanti Wiskemann
Photo: Gabriele Basilico/Abitare

and with numerous shimmering surfaces.

The ceiling may become a decorative element by the use of simple color and texture. Some people re-create intricate carving effects by hiring artists to duplicate the texture and material that used to encrust the spaces overhead. Others ask paperhangers to install ceiling papers which also duplicate, at a considerably reduced cost, the carved patterns that we have once again come to admire.

Often decoration does not wish to imitate the past, only to learn from its lessons.

What might have been a painstakingly drawn mural in another time—designed to add color and texture overhead—may now be replaced by a simple design that coordinates with an uncluttered modern interior.

A few years ago the impulse was to cover up the old ceiling with a system of recessed lights that shrank the room and gave it the appearance of luminous swiss cheese. Now the opposite seems to be true. The old beams, treasured as fragments of history, highlighted by textured

finishes and paint, are often supplemented with new false beams which create a strong sculptural effect overhead.

The periodic rediscovery of tents and the soft, cozy interiors these may have provided show up in the use of decorative fabrics on ceilings and walls. Whether the fabric is shirred or taut, patterned or plain, it continues to be a most popular decorative material which may change its color and tailoring as quickly as the garments that often inspire it or it may remain stylish for many years.

The strong pattern made by the overhead beams is exposed and emphasized by the use of rough plaster with an integral paint applied in the manner of Renaissance frescoes. The same color has been brought down to the upper walls, which are separated, like the sky from the earth on the horizon, at a four-foot nine-inch height, by a fine line of acid-etched copper, recessed into the plasterwork. These subtle touches update such traditional tools of decoration as the plaster wall, the dado, and the chair rail.
Architect: Steven Holl
Photography: Paul Warchol

A round house, built in the manner of African tribal villages, is softened by the liberal use of silk fabric on the walls and the ceiling.
Design: Jack Lenor Larsen
Photography: Paul Warchol

ORNAMENTATION
The Floor

In addition to being the most heavily used surface in the house, the floor can be the major source of ornament in a room. And when the choice of materials is made in response to the activities which gravitate toward each area, the fit between a room and the people who use it has that hard-to-define but instinctively felt rightness about it.

An evaluation of activities leads to choices of floor coverings which are soft or resilient or hard. These may be textured or sleek, quiet to walk on or may mark the act of moving about by giving back its sounds. The material must provide safe passage, good appearance over time, and ease of maintenance.

In open areas, where rooms flow into one another with little or no obstruction, the floor is an essential decorative element which establishes the overall feeling with color and pattern.

The floor chosen for each area defines its function while creating an overview of the open space. The pinks and grays used throughout are warm companions to the humble pine boards. The kitchen and dining area, beyond the fireplace wall, is set on a tile floor with a border design. The same motif, in the same material, this time smaller in area, is repeated in front of the fireplace.

The flat-woven wool rug repeats the colors of the tile "rugs" in a different pattern. It gathers about it the soft sitting group of two 1930s armchairs, two quilted couches, shelving, and a large table, all made in the same unassuming colors.

The pine boards and the inset tiles have in common their subtle speckled patterns, and sun-warmed colors.
Architecture: Carlo Santi
Photography: Gabriele Basilico/ Abitare

In author Geoffrey Archer's London flat the rhythm of movement is aided by the pattern of black-and-white tiles, laid in a strong Mondrianesque grid.
Photography: Morley von Sternberg

Although the room is furnished sparely but with highly decorative pieces, in keeping with its Spanish traditions, the major ornamental element is the black-and-white tile flooring, which has an international appeal.
Photography: Robert Harding Picture Library

The octagon shape of the room becomes the motif of the decorative design of the carpet, which is simply a combination of two strong colors that dominate the library.
Photography: Tim Street-Porter/ EWA

In a pristine white setting that distinguishes itself from its lush South Florida landscape, a surprising splash of color meets the eye. The floor of an open porch is decorated with traditional ceramic tiles, laid as an intricate pattern which resembles a fancy Spanish rug.
Architecture: Julio Gabriel of Spillis, Candela and Partners
Photography: Steven Brooke

The house as a sculpture for living uses everyday materials, which are machined and painted to make a composition filled with decorative detail. The slim wood posts have the same stepped-up pattern as the slate-colored walls and the green insets of the glass wall which correspond to the movement implied by the stairs.
Architecture: Hank Koning and
Julie Eizenberg
Photography: Tim Street-Porter

Restraint is a pleasant companion to ornament. It tests the imagination even as ornament satisfies the need for pattern and color. The gridded door, set demurely into the corner of the powerful white stucco walls is a decorative detail of the first order. The boldly painted overhang, with its plain sculptured shape, issues a clear invitation to move indoors even as it urges the body to continue exploring the exterior shapes and colors from other angles.
Architecture: Luis Barragán
Photography: Allen Carter

ORNAMENTATION

The Building Detail

Ornament and decoration are words which bring to mind the occupations of slower-moving, craft-oriented cultures. The fluted column, the intricate carving, the delicate inlay are commercial rarities today, even if we talk about the revival of craftsmanship.

But far from being outdated, these two words have come into new use. Architects, looking for ways to liven up the basic box for living, are applying fragments of decoration that might have been inspired by Roman pediments, Gothic rosettes, and Colonial gateposts. Used as purely decorative details, these pieces of history might be made of fast-setting polymers, which are poured into molds and finished to look classical or medieval or early American.

Another attitude toward ornament and decoration is occupied less with the imitation of past styles and more with creating a new aesthetic compatible with our own time and technologies. Often this means the use of humble materials like paint, wood, metal, and stucco, shaped in ways

which give buildings the distinctive look of modern sculptures.

Perhaps more than any other art form, modern sculpture seems to announce the separation of art from life, building from ornament. As intensely private statements will do, these artistic expressions often baffle the observer, reinforcing feelings of disconnection between human beings. But like so many things and events around us, modern sculpture may be filled with meanings. And the freedom of imagination it allows—indeed, demands—has come to be part of its special appeal.

An abstract form by a famous artist may be displayed purely as a decorative piece which calls attention to the social status of the people who were discerning enough to buy it at great expense. It may also trigger personal memories and associations which add a richness to the moment.

Be it funny or fantastic, earnest or frivolous, historically significant or of the moment, a sculpture, like other products of the imagination, has the potential of bringing us closer to one another, in thought, when we are receptive to its mysterious message.

Artist Peter Shire has built a little hut on his Los Angeles terrace. To the neighbors it may be a decorative alternative to the barbecue, but for those brought up on the fantasy of Hollywood, this is a sculpture full of associations between the real and the artificial, the natural and the plastic.
Photography: Tim Street-Porter

The ornamental half column, placed on a pedestal inside a pool of gently rippling water, recalls the symbolism of life-giving fountains in ancient courtyard houses inside a new courtyard which itself is a memory.
Architecture: Batey and Mack
Photography: Tim Street-Porter

The bright red assembly of slim metal spokes is in keeping with the lush tropical colors of the energetic plant life of South Florida.
Photography: Steven Brooke

COLLECTIONS

The Best of Everything

Some say that collecting is a search—through material acquisitions—for the self. Since this is a never-ending occupation of each human life, it's not surprising that in materialist cultures, where a plethora of objects abounds, more and more people become collectors.

Those who gather things around them with care and love often talk about the uniqueness of their discoveries, the importance of each piece in relation to the others, the historical significance these may have, the pleasures of the hunt, the find, and the possession. Few resolute collectors ever mention monetary values, but their objects speak for themselves clearly.

A collection can teach its masters about a subject and reveal the lives of other people who were, or still are, involved with it. It does this by example. Those whose lives and work revolve around the subject of design, for instance, find their collections of furnishings and art objects indispensable teachers about form, material, color, texture, and pattern.

The two architects who put furnishings back into the house, Robert Venturi and Denise Scott Brown, talk about the contents of their home as a "teaching collection." She says that they like to have the things "where we can look at them very often and learn from them."

The house itself, an eloquent amalgam of two historical styles—English Arts and Crafts and the later German Jugendstil—receives with generosity the Venturi collection. Samples of the best and most influential designs in decorative arts history are gathered here. It's a case of artists' cohabiting with their muses.

The Venturis' library teaches how a careful examination of seemingly alien styles can lead to discoveries of related details in each and how these can be combined into completely fresh expressions. The eighteenth-century English side chair's unique back splat, for instance, has a disk motif which relates to the 1964 Roy Lichtenstein lithograph's benday-dot pattern, both of which have been picked out by the Venturis' intricate stencilwork on the walls. In the room the stencil pattern spans centuries of design history with great freedom and imagination. The elongated rose bushes after the early twentieth-century Viennese artist Gustav Klimt, the classically inspired urns and stripes of eighteenth-century architect Robert Adam, and the cheerful flowers from 1950s wallpapers are topped with an everlasting symbol of human aspiration: the star-studded heavens.

The Venturi living room, its architecture revealing its 1910 origin, is a comfortable gathering of design history. The freshly stenciled walls, the sunny windows, and the decorative woodwork combine a surprising number of patterns with obvious ease. Here we study Art Nouveau in its various national expressions: the 1902 French marquetry cabinet, the American Tiffany floor lamp, and the German-inspired moldings of the windows. Then Josef Hoffmann's 1911 design for a channel-tufted armchair, which is reproduced in an orange velvet and the delightful ceramic pieces made by another Vienna Sezession artist. The intermingling of Art Nouveau and Art Deco is embodied by the plum-colored velvet club chair and the sofa, which the Venturis acquired from Atlantic City's erstwhile Traymore Hotel of 1915. The orange plastic stacking chair represents the Italian furniture industry's far-reaching expressions in the 1960s, in particular the work of Joe Colombo. The American Andy Warhol's lithograph of "Liz" on the dining room wall also speaks to that decade's attitude toward art and its production. The only missing object is Robert Venturi's 1966 book, Complexity and Contradiction in Architecture, which has made such a room possible once more.

Proving that collectors of great vision are able to integrate seemingly unrelated objects, the Venturis display a plexi maquette for Las Vegas's Desert Inn sign and a Lite Beer neon without disturbing the demure dance of the porcelain sylphs.
Architecture: Robert Venturi and Denise Scott Brown
Photography: Paul Warchol

Dating from about 1910, the handsome Art Nouveau china cabinet in black wood and pewter trimmings encourages diners, with its densely lettered sign, to "Eat Drink and Be Merry."

The contemporary chrome and glass table is perfectly at ease with the floral motif of the Art Nouveau vases and objects, which, in turn, seem to be the older relatives of the 1960s plastic chairs by Joe Colombo. The tall, angular chair was designed in the early 1970s by architect Jon Walleans, who is frankly indebted to the style of the great Scottish Art Nouveau architect Charles Rennie Mackintosh.

A collector's trained eye will pick out a dominant color or a similarity in line in objects which, to others, may seem quite unrelated in style. Such a sensibility is capable of integrating art and life in a home that serves both and does it with great elegance and grace.

A fine, thin line flows through the history of twentieth-century design. In a London flat, originally built at the turn of the century, in a setting which revives typical Edwardian colors—black for the floors; cream for the walls, doors, and silk curtains—architect Jon Walleans gathers together an exquisite collection of twentieth-century objects, all of which have a sinewy tautness about them.

The 1920s, that great era of modern design activity, is represented with the bent-steel works of Marcel Breuer (his famous Wassily chair, which is slung with black leather) and Eileen Gray (her recently revived adjustable end table with a glass top).
Architecture: Jon Wealleans
Photography: Richard Bryant

This Long Island, New York, living room, with its enormous glass walls and metal railings, itself an elegant expression of the International Style, which developed from the thinking of the early twentieth century, is furnished like an exquisite European apartment of the 1920s. A traditional gathering of amply proportioned sofas and club chairs by Ruhlmann is accented by the more angular and delicate wood pieces by Hoffmann.
Photography: Norman McGrath

The enormous chimney breast, with its sculpted wall, green tint, and soaring marlin, surrounded by metal railings of the interior balconies and windows to the upper rooms, promise exalting possibilities—the emotional legacy of the International Style. In this setting the furniture becomes a highly decorative reminder of modern traditions.
Photography: Paul Warchol

COLLECTIONS

The Modern Tradition

A collection may be one of ideas. These, as if by magic, have a way of showing themselves in objects which come to represent a strength of conviction, a thoughtful consideration of how life and art can serve each other. A time when such things were produced was the first quarter of the twentieth century. Everything we do today, every style we find interesting and fresh had their beginnings then.

In Vienna and Paris new modes of gracious and civilized living were being designed in the workshops of Josef Hoffmann and Emile-Jacques Ruhlmann. Called, respectively, Wiener Werkstätte and Art Deco, the two urbane and elegant styles represented a modern sensibility that would not tolerate the heavily encrusted, overworked designs of the previous century. This was what starting a new century looked like. It was an idea whose time had come.

Even as hindsight might declare an era a golden age and some talk wistfully of its return, an astute collector can re-create its spirit while living in his own time. The house built for such a person and such a collection must, of principle, integrate the ideas of sixty years ago with those of today.

Like the elegant lounges of the legendary ocean liners, which were truly "machines for living" and which inspired so much of landbound architecture, the furniture becomes a point of stability, truly a place to retreat from the larger world.
Architecture: Gwathmey Siegel
Photography: Norman McGrath

The fifties pink with its abstract pattern decorates the sectional sofa; its eighties version is slung on two delicate-looking but sturdy chairs, which learned their lessons of form and support from the decade of wide-ranging experiments when the use of metal became an important material in the household.

COLLECTIONS

The Fifties Memory

The decade when chairs looked like potato chips, coffee tables resembled amoebas, and sofas twisted like taut sausages is fondly remembered, mostly by those who were too young to live through it. While to some the 1950s represent a time when production outstripped imagination, to others its distinctive decorative style means a fresh appeal, a new inspiration.

Encouraged by movies, made by people who like to romanticize the time as an age of innocence—their own youth—before the harsh realities—adulthood—of the 1960s set in, the new nostalgia revives a style which seemed dull at the time and gives it a new trendy look.

Spindly furniture is bought from the Salvation Army or re-created with great imagination by a new generation of young designers who are charmed by the forms and colors of their parents' youth. Levittown comes of age.

Tea and coffee sets and glassware recall the time when the coffee klatch was the only connection suburban housewives had with other adults.

The free-form abstractions of the fifties and the popularity of barstools in homes are recalled, as are the decorative qualities of thin metal shapes and meshes in this charming corner.
Design: Kim Milligan
Photography: Tim Street-Porter

The collagelike atmosphere which comes from integrating many diverse but stylistically alike objects is reinforced by the intentionally naïve paper collage in a niched wall.

Living with a teaching collection is as much fun as watching Minnie and Mickey Mouse cavort on the large screen. The completely white living room with its surround of soft cushions and its wall of mirror, is punctuated by the two spindly banana-shaped yellow tables. The many Disney characters are gathered on a rug found in a Milan toyshop. The ubiquitous plastic fruit arrangement is typical of the fifties, and the two reproductions of Gerrit Rietveld's revolutionary 1918 red/blue chair are cushioned with images of other superheroes.

In the bedroom, two barbershop chairs and a trim platform bed stand in contrasting simplicity with dancing Mickey and Minnie statuettes, a store dummy in beach attire about to kick a polka-dot ball, and the suffering heroine of an enlarged comic-strip image.

COLLECTIONS

The Memento

American images of popular culture, produced in such great abundance from the 1950s onward, have influenced the way people live and think all over the world. Technology and its mass production brought the good life to unprecedented numbers of us, with the aid of aggressively marketed consumer items.

While much is made in architectural circles about the importance and decline of the International Style, which is often best represented in the glass and steel skyscraper—that very powerful masculine

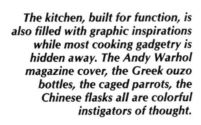

Colorful plastic strips separate the kitchen from the dining room, adding another populist touch of decoration to the room.

The kitchen, built for function, is also filled with graphic inspirations while most cooking gadgetry is hidden away. The Andy Warhol magazine cover, the Greek ouzo bottles, the caged parrots, the Chinese flasks all are colorful instigators of thought.

symbol of heroic materialism fathered by multinational corporations—there are less self-conscious and much more "fun" representatives of other international styles, created by consumer items, like the fantasy world of the Disney cartoon.

In a McLuhanesque "global village" it's not surprising to find the characters of Disneyland as at home in the conservative Swedish town of Malmö as they are at their world headquarters located in Anaheim, California.

Collecting the memorabilia of pop culture is especially important to two designers—the Swedish Gittan and the Italian Nicco—who make their living with the street-smart style popularized by shops like Fiorucci. For them, each new acquisition is an inspiration, another reach into a new wave of imagination that gives their work a distinctive look, which will one day undoubtedly be revived as the eighties style.

The simple easy-to-take-care-of bathroom is punctuated with touches of color like the red-and-black fixtures and the fantasy images of action comics, where a superhero might blindly dive into the toilet tank.

Achille Castiglioni's arc lamp of the 1960s acts like a chandelier over the dining table, which is surrounded by bent-steel chairs with a design date preceding the lamp by thirty years. The gray china cabinet blends into the color of the gray-painted beige-bordered dado around the room. The little boy with the raccoon cap in the leisure wear is part of the plastic still-life collection that inhabits this room.

The contents of an American five-and-dime store on Main Street seem to have been bought out and shipped to Sweden. The charming collection includes a talking alarm clock whose Batman and Robin move time at superspeeds, statuettes of young men and women in their Sunday best visiting the Empire State Building, a neon milk shake, a basketful of plastic fruits, fishes, and ice cream cones, sleek and fuzzy versions of cacti. A highly detailed image of a pineapple decorates the corners of the dining room ceiling, which, like the dado around the walls, updates a centuries-old decorative idea.
Design: Nicco and Gittan
Photography: Lars Kaslow/Abitare

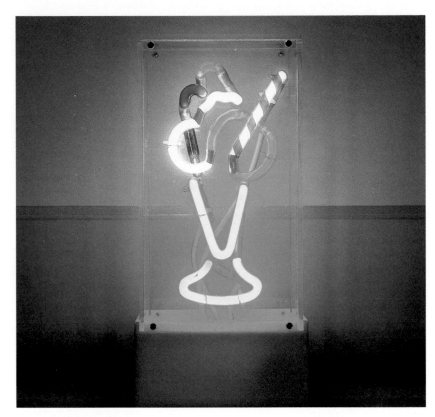

COLLECTIONS
Americana

Enthusiastic collectors whose keen eyes pick out a rare find at a flea market, a garage sale, a barn, or even in a city dumpster are faced with the challenge of living with their burgeoning acquisitions. Whether they decide to become dealers who invite clients to their homes or simply like to rotate items from time to time, for their own pleasure, the spaces that contain these passions are put under constant strain.

One New York City couple, whose love of Americana became a lucrative business, integrates the fruits of their forages with their daily living. Their white-painted rooms receive the ever-changing furniture and decorative items with generosity. Shelves, ledges, consoles, radiator covers, and walls are used to make attractive groupings. Here, the visitor who comes to dinner and covets a decoy duck or the oak table may well end up going home with more than fond memories of good food and company.

The only decoration in the room is a subtle band of stenciling at cornice level, reinforcing the Americana theme. The shallow shelves receive small collectibles; the window niche with its lush plants is used for larger items, and the oriental rug anchors whatever table happens to occupy the room. The flexible track lights can be aimed at the most recent acquisition; while the closed storage under the shelving and the window holds the pieces that have not yet become "hot" on the market.
Photography: Paul Warchol ©
ESTO

Thinly cut slabs of slate, tinted in the same color as the carpet, combine the decorative idea of a traditional chair rail with the utilitarian idea of shelving. Its minimal form implies minimal display. The few items are placed casually, in turn implying a freedom to change, as does the placement of the white ladder, a sculpture by Bruce Robbins which leans against the wall.
Design: Kevin Walz
Photography: Peter Vitale

One painting out of a collection of many is highlighted by its placement on the expansive white wall. The others lean against the wall in layers. Prints, folios, paintings, and sculptures line the traditional church stand. Such casual arrangement of valuable possessions implies a constant, personal interaction with them; the several layers can be rotated by the curious hand.
Architecture: Luis Barragán
Photography: Allen Carter

COLLECTIONS
The Display

Collecting presents the problem of placement and display. The items of value and pleasure must be sufficiently visible to inform the world about us of our special interest, our finely honed taste, our unique ability to make intelligent choices. All these, represented by the things we keep around us, show others that we are creative people, in a world that considers the act of choosing as creative as the act of making.

Some people prefer to keep only a few items on selective display, leaving them out until their eyes grow indifferent to them, then to store these away and bring out a few pieces which will look refreshingly new for a while, repeating this cycle of renewal endlessly.

Others like to have everything they own public, giving it every available surface, building special containers to highlight interesting arrangements which might be made by type, size, color, pattern, historical significance as well as other, more personal reasons.

For still others, the handling of a collection gives a special pleasure. Its daily maintenance gives them an opportunity to reinforce feelings of ownership and control. Such highly personal collections tend to be off limits to other members of the household, who may admire but never touch a single item without permission.

Each piece of sculpture or ceramic is highlighted in its own niche, which is scaled to the artwork's dimension. Thus, each may be enjoyed separately for its own sake or celebrated together as a unique collection of riches.
Design: Dennis Jenkins
Photography: Steven Brooke

Attention must be paid to the delightful ceramic menagerie housed in its own illuminated carved-out niche. The interior of the niche, the front of the cabinet doors below are indicated by the change of scale in the wallpaper pattern and the application of a border design.
Design: Gaie Lee
Photography: Clive Helm/EWA

On an inset wall, lit by recessed fixtures, etchings are neatly lined up over a built-in credenza, where a few, equally linear pieces of sculpture are on display. Each picture tells a visual story while its legend may be read for more specific information.
Design: Armando Valdez
Photography: Steven Brooke

Transparent glass shelves are lined with a delicate shell collection. Such an open display requires constant maintenance though it provides endless delights in the discovery of nature's colors, patterns, and textures by the devoted collector.
Photography: Neil Lorimer/EWA

The perfect wall, which seems to have been made for a painting, calls attention to a valued possession even in a room which is chock-full of other ideas beckoning from the hundreds of book spines that line the walls.
Design: Smith and Thompson
Photography: Norman McGrath

Like a jeweler's case, an antique piece of velvet highlights a collection of precious stones which require constant handling, arranging, matching, and studying and just marveling at what wonders time and the elements can create with simple materials.
Design: Paul Anstee
Photography: Michael Dunne/EWA

A symmetrical arrangement of similarly-patterned and shaped plates on the wall is continued on the couch, where many small handmade pillows are grouped around the largest one.
Design: Leila Corbette
Photography: Michael Nicholson/ EWA

A delicately ornamented antique cabinet, painted in richly contrasting colors, is a perfect showcase for a collection of fancy-dress ceramic figurines and ornate china.
Photography: Neil Lorimer/EWA

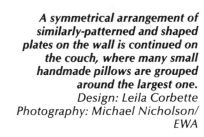

A collection of many different items, each very much a visual relative of the other but representing many different ways of handling materials, makes an interesting corner of wonders that never stays the same.
Design: Jon Wealleans
Photography: Richard Bryant

LIGHTING, HEATING, AND COOLING

How we choose to conduct our daily lives in our homes has taken on a significance far beyond style and status. Survival—of ourselves, our communities, our ecosystems, our earth—seems to be at stake. We receive, via satellite, global reports of blackouts, poisoned aquifers, and acid rain. And even minor mechanical failures—when light, temperature, water, or information is interrupted—may briefly turn our comfortable homes into major sources of frustration and inconvenience. The hidden systems of wires, conduits, ducts, and pipes have turned us into more vulnerable creatures than our ancestors who only feared "being at the mercy of nature."

With this realization comes the new thinking about living in the late twentieth century. Passive solar buildings—the natural mode of architecture for centuries before mechanization took command—are under new consideration. This involves an evaluation of site and weather conditions, vegetation, and materials. All these work to produce a house which relies more on nature, and on us, as its intelligent creatures than merely on our technologies. Our homes are beginning to reflect our growing need to take back some control over our own lives.

So mechanical systems, which were designed to override what nature on its own accord has always given freely, are now under scrutiny. But more significantly, our need for these systems is also being questioned. As a result, lighting, heating, and cooling the house have become important issues of design. The new look is often a result of studying the location of the house as well as the interior spatial divisions in terms of local realities and individuals' real needs.

For the interior, this can mean a look at each opening in each room in terms of the light and heat it may bring in or take out. Thus, the quality and quantity of light through the window determine its placement, shape, and fenestration.

The desire to rely less on central heating and cooling is also producing a change in the look and feel of the house. Baseboard heating systems with their even temperatures are analyzed in terms of our needs for change and variety, which are innate to us as creatures of nature. The sealed glass wall is giving way to many different-size operable windows, such as the ones located high up where a ceiling fan turns with the natural breezes and the two together keep the air moving and fresh.

The placement of masonry walls—known in solar language as "trombe" walls—behind a sandwich of south-facing glass adds radiant heat to the interior during the winter months, when the foliage from the surrounding trees no longer blocks the heat of the sun.

The addition of fireplaces and cast-iron and ceramic-tile stoves has brought back the friendly glow and the steady heat of tradition and updated these with efficient fuel use. Romantic descriptions from history by authors and architects whose work is being reconsidered are expanding our thinking about the basic need for keeping warm as well as adding a new set of tools and chores for various members of the family.

Edith Wharton, with her nineteenth-century reliance on domestic help, and Frank Lloyd Wright, with his traditional views on women's work, could dream, respectively, of living rooms with inglenooks, where the crackling fire is "an active participant of family life," or feel comforted upon seeing "the fire burning deep in the solid masonry of the house." Today's commitment to finding alternative ways of living and using resources gives a new realistic interpretation to such sentimental notions.

Windows bring in light from above, from the side, adding the element of time to the interior. Breeze from on high gently turns the ceiling fans, which keep the air fresh. The two Luxo lamps clamped to tables built around a cozy seating next to the fire illuminate a reader's task as the flames warm the body.
Architecture: Stanley Tigerman and Margaret McCurry
Photography: Karant + Associates

LIGHTING

The Window

Light may catch the sparkle of glass one moment, brighten a color the next, and reveal a niche which moments before was obscured in shadow. Such dynamic vision of an interior is made possible by designing openings to capture the moment's mood. These accesses to the exterior record the position of the sun, the density of the cloud cover, and the movement of the foliage, all of which change with the hour, the day, the season.

Because of the new interest in integrating time and space with architecture, the window has taken on many shapes which were forgotten for a while. Now we seek out the sliver of sunlight that dapples the walls from a strip window in the eaves, the floods of illumination which rush in through the skylight, the mist that filters through a hidden opening.

We instinctively place lamps near the natural source of light, asking these fixtures with their dimmers and hoods and screened bulbs and adjustable necks to mime the sun till it appears once more.

The breaking down of boundaries between exterior and interior, of integrating the house completely with its natural environment was being explored with great success during the 1950s by one of this century's most influential architects, Ludwig Miës van der Rohe. The window is a wall is a screen is a garden. The glass walls and wire-mesh screens glide out of the way, opening the inside completely to the outside when the party gets going by the newly added swimming pool.
Architecture: Peter Gluck
Photography: Paul Warchol

The ever-changing seascape is framed in a romantic medallion-shaped window which highlights its interior surroundings with great delicacy.
Architecture: Graham Gund Assoc.
Photography: Steve Rosenthal

Light from a thin slit in the ceiling moves across the wall and floor as the sun travels its daily course. Filtered through the wooden beams, the dappled light adds a feeling of warmth to the kitchen without its Southern California heat.
Architecture: Hank Koning and
Julie Eizenberg
Photography: Tim Street-Porter

A small space under the eaves is used as a source of light which comes from a triangular clerestory. Night light comes from the same direction as the reflector lamps on the cornice are activated.
Architecture: Eric Owen Moss
Photography: Tim Street-Porter

Light entering the adjacent bathroom is filtered and faceted by the bedroom's interior windows of glass block. This device expands the space with light, creates a "front" for the room, and gives it an ever-changing pattern of decorative surfaces. The lamps above duplicate the daytime source of light for nighttime activities.
Architecture: Eric Owen Moss
Photography: Tim Street-Porter

A golden light invades a narrow hallway through an inset window where yellow paint imitates the sun's glow. The thick protective walls guard against the Mexican sun's penetrating heat.
Architecture: Luis Barragán
Photography: Allen Carter

The Skylight

"The best way to light a house is God's way," said Frank Lloyd Wright. So what can be more natural than a skylight which brings the very source of divine illumination, the heavens, into the house? Although such notions are often dismissed as mere emotion, the fact remains that human beings are enlivened by the sun. Remember the last spell of overcast days and the progressive decline of spirits, followed by the sudden joy of bright sunshine?

Whether it's a dome, a clerestory, or a funnel, the skylight animates the interior space with its illumination. We move toward it, bask in it, linger, and come alive.

Mysterious or obvious, this light can paint patterns on the floor, force a sharp shaft of sunshine through a dusky space, bathe the adjacent rooms in pearly iridescence, and provide many other surprises which are expressions of a basic human instinct to live in light.

Like the Roman villas which inspired it, the atrium of a Texas house illuminates the rooms from above and draws an ever-changing pattern on the travertine floors.
Architecture: Batey and Mack
Photography: Tim Street-Porter

The lightweight wood construction which revolutionized home building—called the balloon frame—is revealed here as the beams and trusses are left open to behave as a natural decorative trellis which filters the light from the clerestory windows.
Architecture: Frank O. Gehry
Photography: Tim Street-Porter

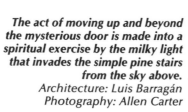

The act of moving up and beyond the mysterious door is made into a spiritual exercise by the milky light that invades the simple pine stairs from the sky above.
Architecture: Luis Barragán
Photography: Allen Carter

A striking diagonal pattern of the latticed shutters chops up the California sunlight into decorative slivers or allows it to enter as pure and unobstructed illumination through the tall window, which is cut to follow the shape of the roofline. The overhead fixture extends the function of the window as a natural light source into the night.
Architecture: Hank Koning and Julie Eizenberg
Photography: Tim Street-Porter

LIGHTING
The Screen

Light is texture. It flows; it ripples; it layers; it pools with the help of intermediary surfaces. The shutter, the shade, the blind, the screen, the curtain bring light in selectively, each in its own way.

Such controlling devices are at their best when they respond to a person's need for closeness or openness, warmth or coolness, light or shadow during the course of the day. A room's use is thus enriched greatly when such barriers between the outside and inside can be freely manipulated. Old-fashioned wooden shutters, for instance, make it possible to flood the room with the new shine of morning, dapple it with warmth during the afternoon, mist it with coolness in the early evening, and cover it up for private moments in the dark of night.

The old-fashioned wooden shutters in a deepset window control light with great virtuosity. They can darken or brighten the room completely as well as allow only slivers of light to enter on occasion. Painted in contrasting blue with the room's earth tones, the window's woodwork is in keeping with the homey feeling of the restored Italian farmhouse's beamed ceiling, stone floor, and sparsely deployed decorative furnishings.
Design: Teresa Pomodoro and Giancarlo Montebello
Photography: Antonia Mulas/ Abitare

Stained glass, a time-tested material for manipulating light, continues to add its decorative beauty to the interior with overdoor lights which bring the soft gray-green of the surrounding pines into the house.
Design: Al Garber
Photography: Robert Perron

A filmy fabric becomes a delightful window ornament which filters the light and adds a classical architectural memory to a modern kitchen with the aid of an appliquéd Ionic column and wooden dowels.
Design: Joy Wulke
Photography: Robert Perron

A double layer of deeply textured fabric is suspended from hinged brackets, which close to obscure light and obstruct passage in the manner of french doors.
Design: Jack Lenor Larsen
Photography: Robert Grant

LIGHTING

The Curtain

"Lingerie effects do not combine well with architecture," warned Edith Wharton at the turn of the century. In her campaign to brighten the stuffy Victorian room, she pointed out that "the more architecturally a window is treated, the less it needs to be dressed in ruffles." Although lush festoons of fabrics with their opaque interlining continue to upholster windows and remain useful protectors against torrid summer days and frigid winter nights, the architecture of the house has all but made these applied decorations obsolete. Double and triple glazing, careful consideration of window placement, size, and fenestration add new controls to the interior light and temperature.

Wharton's warnings have helped create a century of awareness of the window as a light giver. We study the filtering qualities of fabrics which act as intermediaries, not as barriers between the outside and the inside. Of the many materials of choice, each fabric has a natural fall which makes it a unique window treatment. The pearlescent folds of rich silks, the crisp pleating of cottons and linens, the gossamer layering of muslin—all work to create the openness we have come to expect from our rooms.

Cotton muslin, which lines the enveloping windows of an enclosed porch, creates a softly lighted room even on cloudy days and robs the encroaching darkness of its intensity at night. The slim wooden dowels, which give the fabric screens their pattern, also work to make them taut, similar to the translucent architectural membranes of glass.
Design: Joy Wulke
Photography: Robert Perron

Crisp cotton shades drop to make a wall of fabric or pleat up to bring in the foliage-filtered light from the balcony, which extends the livable space of a small Milan apartment.
Design: Mariella Frateili
Photography: Gabriele Basilico/ Abitare

Layers of translucent muslin, sewn together as wave-patterned screens which overlap one another, create a complex play of filtered light and shadow forms at the window.
Design: Joy Wulke
Photography: Robert Perron

LIGHTING

The Glass Wall

With the modern skyscraper came the glass wall and the open space filled with light. But hovering somewhere between heaven and earth, while a decidedly uplifting experience, has required a constant study of how to balance the sometimes harsh environmental conditions with domestic demands for comfort.

While some new skyscrapers are being designed as if they were vertical landscapes, incorporating open atria, terraces, miniforests, and fenestrations, all of which mediate between the exterior and the interior conditions, most modern high-rise apartment residents are faced with the necessity of finding their own controls to gain heat and light.

Interiors which take full advantage of the panoramic views and the constantly changing light delight their occupants with the daily play of hot pinks, warm oranges, cool greens and blues and grays, elegant indigos, and blacks. Intensifying or toning down such experiences is aided by an adjustable system of artificial lights and an astute choice of materials which interact readily with light.

The 1950s Chicago skyscraper built by Miës van der Rohe, the architect known for his elegant use of materials like steel, glass, and anodized aluminum, contains a 1980s style apartment which uses the materials of technology with great ease and sophistication even as it accepts light as its chief source of decoration. The undulating stainless steel ledge, with its built-in heating and cooling systems, imitates the shoreline of Lake Michigan below and establishes a theme of smoothly curving, highly polished forms and surfaces throughout. The curtain wall's glare is subdued by the metal blinds, while the pocket doors which slide behind the illuminated glass walls control the flow of light and aid privacy in the open space.

Thin, perforated aluminum sheets are cut in a wave pattern and layered to filter with varying intensities the light which enters the glass-enclosed dining area. The layering and texture created by these screens are imitated in the decorative patterns of the ceiling and floor, rendered, like the other surfaces, in highly polished automotive paints. The furniture—except the chairs—like the building, is bolted-down metal and glass.

The living area's light is balanced by the glass block walls which have been made into colossal lighting fixtures on dimmers. The velvet and satin upholstery fabrics take on the hues reflected from the windows.

The red highlights of the dining area cast a warm glow over the glass-enclosed room, the chief decorative element of which is the light from the windows and the electrified glass block walls.
Architecture: Krueck and Olsen
Photography: © Bill Hedrich/
Hedrich-Blessing

LIGHTING
The Lamp

A lamp is simply a light giver, a device which gives us the ability to see and be seen, to hold back the dark. But there's nothing simple about the lamp in either use or meaning. Its placement, its shape, its intensity, its color and texture rendition, its ability to be controlled by dimmers, switches, filters, and movable parts, and its interaction with others of its kind make the lamp one of the most challenging objects of interior design. Add to these our romantic notions about the lamp, defined by Webster's dictionary as "a heavenly body...a source of intellectual and spiritual illumination," and the question of choosing the lighting to fit the activities in each area of the house turns out to be complex indeed.

Things get further complicated when we study photographs of rooms. These are useful in learning about the placement of lamps, their shapes and materials, but the quality of light they create in a room can be experienced only by being there. For what may look like a truly seductive room, where the light sparkles on the rich woodwork and crystal, collects in warm pools around objects of desire, and dapples the walls and ceilings through the arrested tremble of ficus leaves, is actually a highlighted image made by the photographer's lights, which dramatize existing conditions.

Milky glass balls over the picture rails and hidden in niches by the window give a festive uplift to a London dining room where the position of honor is marked by the fancy chair and the pink-masked lamp which adds a healthy glow to complexions.
Photography: Morley von Sternberg

The Milanese light which floods in from all sides during the day is remembered at night, conservatively, by the two gray aluminum hoods which are fixed on high, near the gray-painted panels of the ceiling's plane.
Design: Yolanda Collamanti Wiskemann
Photography: Gabriele Basilico/ Abitare

The swiveling ceiling lamps which light the kitchen beyond the partial wall add their glow to the hanging lamp placed, off center, over the dining table. The wiring on the exposed beam ceiling creates a decorative mesh pattern overhead, repeating the sinewy lines of the forms throughout the sparely furnished room.
Architecture: Hank Koning and Julie Eizenberg
Photography: Tim Street-Porter

While some designers argue that lighting fixtures are "unnatural" objects which were never meant to simulate the sun, others admit to learning a great deal about artificial light by studying the ever-changing values of natural light and our responses to both. When several different fixtures are combined in a room, it's possible to add or subtract light and change its direction according to the needs of people who gather there.

In our public rooms a variety of lighting conditions sets the moods for the many interactions that are likely to happen. The sparkle and brightness which accompany festive occasions, the dusky half-light for quiet conversations, the even wash of light for brisk businesslike contacts, the soft surround of light for encouraging new friendships, as well as many other possibilities for memorable human contact, are helped along by the fixtures we choose.

The sunburst shape of the standing lamps was designed as a replica of the California sun, though that heavenly orb is rarely this gentle in those parts. Their rippled white glass shades protect the eye from glare and wash the ceiling in a soft white light which reflects on the surrounding white surfaces. The white track lights on the beam direct their own beams of light below when the white-shaded table lamp's friendly pool of light needs assistance.
Architecture: Charles Jencks and Buzz Yudell
Photography: Tim Street-Porter

The city lights and textures which surround many a lower Manhattan loft provide an ambience that is hard to imitate by interior lighting fixtures. One way to capitalize on such fortunate givens is by the restrained use of lamps which soften the glitter with their milky shades. These angular forms update traditional standing lamps in the same way that the ingeniously joined wooden chairs and glass-top table define a new urban sensibility.
Design and Photography: James Evanson

Rooms that are mostly used at night provide unique stages for lighting. The surrounding darkness signals a slowing of pace, a separation of the public and private. It's time to replenish the spirit, refresh the body, get ready for the activities of the next sunrise.

Such personal rooms contain activities which require various intensities of lighting: a clear and balanced light for dressing and undressing; a comfortable, glare-free spot which directs itself on a book's page without casting its reflection on reading glasses; a soft light which balances the blue haze of the TV screen; a mysteriously indirect light which warms and sparkles intimate moments; and convenient switches for safe passage to and from the room.

Light comes from three major sources, combining the different activities of this small New York bedroom. From the two openings cut into the partial wall which divides dressing and sleeping areas, the light comes into the bedroom as if from two high windows. These and the lamp over the window provide the overall lighting. The two standing goosenecks welcome the reader at either end of the bed. The materials chosen add to the intimate mood of the room. The shiny walls reflect enigmatic shadows; the "oil-slick" color of the silk on the oak daybed and the orange-color silk balloon shade give a warm shimmer all around.

The bookshelves, conveniently located near the bed are built of corrugated aluminum, the material from which airplanes are made. Their shiny surfaces and rippled edges sparkle and call attention to the books.
Design: Kevin Walz
Photography: Peter Vitale

At times when its light is not needed, a lamp functions as a purely decorative object. As such, it is required to be in aesthetic agreement with the other furnishings in the room to echo the linear, material, and formal qualities of the objects with which it shares the space.

The source of light, the bulb, has changed a great deal in recent years. This technological development is reflected in the shape of the lamp. As a result, the lamp has become one of the most interesting objects in home furnishings. Its very essence has come to represent those ever-present occupations of modern times: the integration of art with technology and easy mobility.

A small clip-on lamp, which can fasten anywhere along the pine-plank headboard and table of the bed, expands the possibilities for comfortable reading. The metal fixture is as unpretentious and as emotionally appealing as the more traditional furnishing items like the wool rug and the simple bedding.
Architecture: Carlo Santi
Photography: Gabriele Basilico/ Abitare

The invention of the tiny light bulb had made possible a new generation of slim, adjustable lamps like Richard Sapper's trend-setting Tizio, a 1972 design which combines the industrial materials of plastic and aluminum with great wit and elegance. That it's in such harmony with objects which clearly bear the mark of other times continues to make this lamp a refreshing addition to rooms furnished in many different styles.
Architecture: Jon Wealleans
Photography: Richard Bryant

Even when it's not needed to cast its soft light upward and onto the shiny surfaces which surround it, the turtlelike floor lamp is a comfortable companion to several decades of decorative expression which share a spirit of simple color, sculptured form, and smooth texture.
Architecture: Jon Wealleans
Photography: Richard Bryant

Although the choice of available lighting fixtures has expanded greatly during the past few years, architects and designers, in search of a unified aesthetic, continue to devise their own unique lamps. While few of these may be put into production, most remain rare pieces of sculpture, which are often valued by their owners as such. The value increases as the architects' fame grows.

The current crop of fixtures provides a clue to the chief design trends of the mid-1980s. These explore traditional ideas about placement, material, and detail in highly romantic ways, in styles as varied as modern, postmodern, and new wave.

The optimistic spirit of the 1950s is captured by designer Kim Milligan's new wave standing lamp, which uses the thin, tough, resilient materials that made starships and skyscrapers and metal-mesh furniture part of our lives.
Photography: Tim Street-Porter

The traditional wall sconce is updated by architect Steven Holl as a simple assemblage of sand-blasted glass wings, metal brackets and a silver-tipped bulb. The fixture's slim, refined lines are in aesthetic harmony with the thin copper reveal, which slices into the plaster wall of the decidedly modern New York interior.
Photography: Paul Warchol

The highly decorative language of postmodern architecture, used by Charles Jencks, the man who coined the term, is expressed in a lamp which makes a romantic reference to California palm trees.
Photography: Tim Street-Porter

HEATING
Hands-On

The nervous television couple whose facial expressions twist into near hysteria with each new rumble of the furnace are, in reality, every homeowner concerned with high heating bills. The fears of being wasteful citizens have encouraged the development of a whole set of new industries which promise to stop the leak of expensive heating dollars at the walls, the roof, the windows, and the floor. In a few short years we've come to understand the importance of the tight weatherskin and of double or triple glazing.

That even heat throughout the house is unnecessary is common knowledge again, forgotten briefly in the years of construction booms and cheap energy. In cold climates, the lessons learned by the New England builders are studied once more. Thus, grouping main areas of activity around the central heating—whether

The wood burning stove on the ground level—which is embedded in the land's gentle slope to contain two south-facing bedrooms and the north-facing bath and utility areas— heats the entire house in Maine. The main floor, an open space made for living, dining, cooking, is brightened and warmed by the unobstructed south-facing windows in addition to the rising heat from below. The loft, which shares the openness of the house through the railing that connects it to the living space below, serves as a study, music room, and playroom for the young couple and their child.
During the summer months, climbing plants on trellises outside the windows shade the interior, while the balcony brings the living room outdoors.
Design: Bentley/LaRosa/Salasky
Photography: Timothy Hursley

this comes from radiators, floorboards, fireplaces, cast-iron stoves, or a combination of systems—has brought new thinking about how we live in our houses.

By cushioning the inner core with a series of lesser-used rooms—be these corridors, closets, or utility and service areas—the harsh exterior temperatures and winds are kept where they belong. The house, so planned, is its own generous protector. Its rooms function the same way as layers of clothing, which trap heat.

For many, such changes imply an intensive "hands-on" policy of chopping the wood, stoking the stove, operating the shutters, and finding materials to soak up the sun's heat during the day and release its warmth at night. For the more technologically inclined, there's a growing number of options made available by the microchip. The totally controlled environment, even in passive solar houses, is now nearing realization. Microprocessors and home computers can be programmed to respond to temperature changes by activating the windows, fans, and heating and lighting systems according to a predetermined standard of comfort.

The warmth which radiates from the cast-iron stove and the metal sheets that back it up and support it circulates freely in the open space. The sun comes in through the skylight and the ample windows, which are guarded by roll-up shades during the summer.
Architecture: Hank Koning and Julie Eizenberg
Photography: Tim Street-Porter

HEATING
The Stove

The cast-iron stove, made in new airtight versions which burn wood with frugal efficiency, has returned to the household. It brings a pleasant, steady heat into rooms where the movement of people and pets mix the warm with the cooler air by a physical process called convection. In high-vaulted rooms, gently turning ceiling fans bring the heat down from the rafters, redirecting it to where the people are.

Amid reports of amazing dollar savings on energy, millions of homeowners have purchased these metal boxes which were not long ago displayed as quaint artifacts in museums of folk art. The stove can either supplement central heating or function as the sole source of cold-weather warmth. The cast-iron stove multiplies household chores and pits itself against the tendency to mechanize. This additional appliance, like much of the thinking about passive solar building, ex-

presses a wish to slow things down, at least in our homes, to a readily understood pace which requires personal participation in the act of living.

Such thinking goes on in neighborhoods where the folks next door may be greeted at the front door by the voice of their computer, which is programmed to distinguish a friendly entrant from an unfriendly intruder, to preheat the house before the expected homecoming, and to activate the lights, the music, and the microwave the moment the master has finished punching in the numbers of the entry code.

Plants and people soak up the sun's heat radiated from the window and from the stored energy of the wood, which is released by the burning fire in the cast-iron stove.
Photography: Franco Ziglioli/ Abitare

The Fireplace

Even with the addition of metal liners and tube grates which are designed to radiate more warmth into the room, less up the chimney, fireplaces remain the least efficient sources of heat. In spite of this, throughout a century of central heating the fireplace has retained its romantic associations with all that we think of as home. Family gatherings and friendships as well as solitary musings seem to benefit from its primeval glow.

Perhaps because the open fire calls attention to all our senses, at a time when experiences seem like mere fragments, we continue to respond to it with renewed enthusiasm. This shows up not only in the immediate pleasure we take as the fire plays with our sight, hearing, touch, and scent but in the creativity we lavish on its container.

Taking advantage of the fireplace's radiant heat, which has a tendency to travel in a direct line, a traditional gathering of nontraditional furniture in a New York apartment pulls the residents close to the fire. The sculptural pyramid of the monumental wall with its angled mirror, niched light, and finely detailed surfaces creates a strong focus for the room, even without the fire.
Architecture: Calvin Tsao
Photography: Paul Warchol

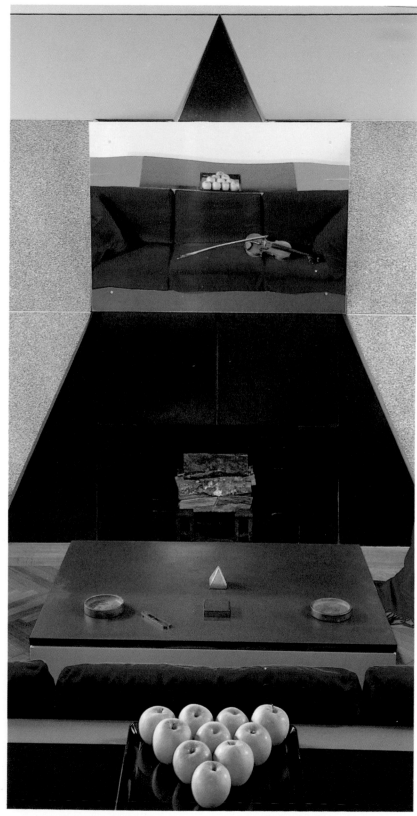

The Ceiling Fan

Air moving through the house, its path marked by the gently rippling fabrics, the buzzing of bees, and the scent of honeysuckle has all but been banished by what we call "comfort." Reliance on the air conditioner has substituted even temperatures and a steady mechanical hum.

When houses were built with a complete disregard for local conditions, the mechanical bias seemed, indeed, to be the only alternative to roasting in stifling interiors. But the new thinking about the importance of working with, instead of against the elements, is adding a new richness to the ways we live.

In hot climates, the natural movement of air is incorporated into the house by the design of high ceilings, floor-to-ceiling windows, which allow cross breezes, screened and shaded porches, protective overhangs, ventilating cupolas and dormers, and surfaces that "breathe."

In climates with extreme seasonal variations, there's an attempt to study and catch the prevailing winds for summer cooling. High placement of windows, which takes out the rising heat, aided by gently turning fans are signs that a new sensibility is at work.

The high, central room onto which balconies open on both sides, built for vacationing in Michigan, is punctuated with regularly-placed, small windows under the roofline which exchange the heated air of the house with the cooler breezes from the surrounding woods, aided by gentle ceiling fans.
Architecture: Stanley Tigerman and Margaret McCurry
Photography: Karant + Associates

The screened porch takes full advantage of seaside light, air, and dunes in the Hamptons of New York. It's a layer of sunny space—cooled by its many openings and low-hanging ceiling fans.
Architecture: Gwathmey Siegel
Photography: Norman McGrath

C H A P T E R • F I V E

LIVING

For much of this century, domestic architecture has been concerned with openness and flexibility. Western thinking has been inspired by the traditional Japanese house that evolved through generations from the simple belief that life is not static. The house—container of human life—therefore needs to be a place that adapts to and changes with the lives of the people who live there. The open, minimally furnished rooms of the Japanese house, with doors and walls functioning as mere screens that slide out of the way, fascinated Frank Lloyd Wright, the most studied architect of the twentieth century. His influence is as far-reaching as the utopian dreams of the 1920s European architects who set out to change the way we live and the American mass builders of the 1950s who succeeded in this by marketing their open-plan split-levels to a house-hungry public.

The quest for openness and flexibility continues to occupy us. But the experiences of the past decades have taught us to pay more attention to our needs for privacy, quiet, and solitude. Architects respond with buildings that push the use of space to its limits. This may be done simply by constructing changes in floor levels and partial walls, which distinguish one area of activity from another. Or the solution may be a complex organization of rooms in an open loft or towerlike structure.

That the Japanese house is part of its garden, which is part of the greater world of nature, is revealed in its openness to its surroundings and in the natural materials that are used throughout. Delight is taken in the irregularities of the wooden shapes and surfaces as well as in the subtle colors, which are chosen for their simple contrasts. These are perceived as the motivating forces for people's actions as well as for their expressions, of which architecture is one. The passageways between the interior rooms, for instance, are marked by their change in scale, level, and textures. This Zen view of integrating opposites into one, easily understood whole is seen in how the building is put together. The supporting structure of the house with its strong uprights and spans of wooden beams is in direct contrast with the delicate, movable screens which separate and connect the rooms and the gardens.

The way we sit and recline has far-reaching significance for the way we furnish our homes. What seems like an empty room in the Japanese house, becomes an animated and highly flexible space where people gather to kneel together on the resilient rush mats (tatami) or roll out thickly wadded quilts (futons) for sleeping, then clear away all this paraphernalia for living by storing it in the surrounding closets. The Western definition of comfort tends to be more centered on luxury, which explains why we buy thick, foam-reinforced futons, heavy metal-sprung mattresses, and bulky chairs even for rooms which have been influenced by the Japanese minimalist traditions.
Photography: Paul Warchol

The main living area with its kitchen and dining space is lifted to the house's third floor, giving it generous views from every direction.

Circulation through the loft space is handled by an open stairway, which is located on the north edge of the obliquely angled vertical shaft of the house.

LIVING

The Tower

"...only one room, a vast, rude, substantial, primitive hall, without ceiling or plastering, with bare rafters..." was what Henry David Thoreau dreamed of on the shores of Walden Pond. Since his influential writings about personal freedoms in the middle of the nineteenth century, the freedom of interior spaces has been as much part of the American dream as upward mobility has been.

This expansive spirit can be captured in one large room for living, which claims a piece of vertical space and organizes the activities therein on several layers, each open to the other. Skylights, clerestories, corner windows, and walls of glass are cut into the house's balloon frame, a type of construction which encourages such freedoms of expression with light. The uniformity of the unpretentious materials that naturally springs from the exposed wooden trusses and beams, which are left in their natural state but protected by a mixture of wood preservative and linseed oil, defines this as a house of one room with many parts.

Jane Spiller, the California filmmaker who lives in this Venice house with views of the Pacific, took an active role in its building by supervising the construction and making sure that the signs of the building process were preserved. With some difficulty, she convinced the contractors that their work had aesthetic qualities, which her trained eyes discovered in such details as the exposed corner beads of the drywall and the red crayon marks left by the plumber.

The bathroom's light, gained from a window over the tub, is transferred by a clerestory window to the bedroom which joins it on the second floor, where the pink wall is washed in a gentle wake-up light from the east.
Architecture: Frank O. Gehry & Associates
Photography: Tim Street-Porter

The dumbwaiter, which connects the living spaces to the garage below, is handy for transporting packages through the vertical room. Its wheels and pulleys have the same kinetic sculptural qualities as the house itself.

LIVING

The Studio

Families with working wives and husbands—often in partnership with one another—depend on mutual nurturing and joint responsibility for taking care of small children and domestic chores. This is reflected by the shape and plan of the home. Apartments which were built for other times and other life-styles, then converted to serve the new ways provide a lesson in human adaptability.

Tall flats that have generous vertical dimensions but small floor spaces are sliced up to add a third or more living area to them, while retaining their attractive openness. An innovative example of this is seen in the London studio of Peter and Julia Wilson, two young architects who live and work in an early Victorian house with tall ceilings and huge windows. By building a bedroom gallery, reached from the office area by a staircase that is so tightly planned that it requires starting off on the right foot, they successfully separated daytime and nighttime functions within the open space. In the main room, where business and family life are conducted, a simple painted block, placed on a diagonal, separates the two zones while signaling the importance of both.

The plain cube of the dining room reveals itself as a storage shelf on the office side. Here the residents' archaeological interests, which are most clearly read in the remnant of the fireplace, are seen on the crossbeam of the pediment, which has been left in its natural state, including the markings from the lumberyard. The small spiky sculptures made by the Wilsons—like far-out interpretations of eggcups—are in aesthetic harmony with the tough little geometric plants on the windowsill.

By keeping furniture down to the most necessary pieces—the Art Deco sideboard, chairs, and table were bought from the Salvation Army; the wooden office chairs were found on a German street— the single room accommodates dining, living, and working without cramping. The painted block suggests that a different room for a different function is concealed behind it.

Decorating the passage to the kitchen is a storage wall which puts the space under the stairs to practical use. The tiny knobs of the drawers, the shimmer of the Japanese paper on the screen of the stairway, the dark oak, and the cool black tile floors combine in a richly decorative scheme with no pretensions to opulence.
Architecture: Peter and Julia Wilson
Photography: Richard Davies

LIVING

The Apartment

Living in densely packed cities has many unique rewards, but often space is not one of these. Those fortunate enough to land in a shoebox with a generous view tend to celebrate this miracle by using the windows as space extenders. Indeed, if the apartment is high enough and the view is unobstructed enough, the interior's small physical dimensions are hardly noticeable.

In a room (twenty-seven feet by fourteen feet) with a wide ribbon of glass that brings in the glorious northern light of midtown Manhattan, designer Lew Dolin lives and works with no sign of crowding. By the use of partial walls, which allow light and air to circulate freely throughout the apartment, aided by built-in furniture and changes in the floor level, the small room becomes a spacious container of integrated functions: living/reception, dining/office, and sleeping/entertainment.

Simply an arrangement of couch, window seat, and two coffee tables, the living room is immensely expanded by its clear view. The pull-up shades are rarely used.

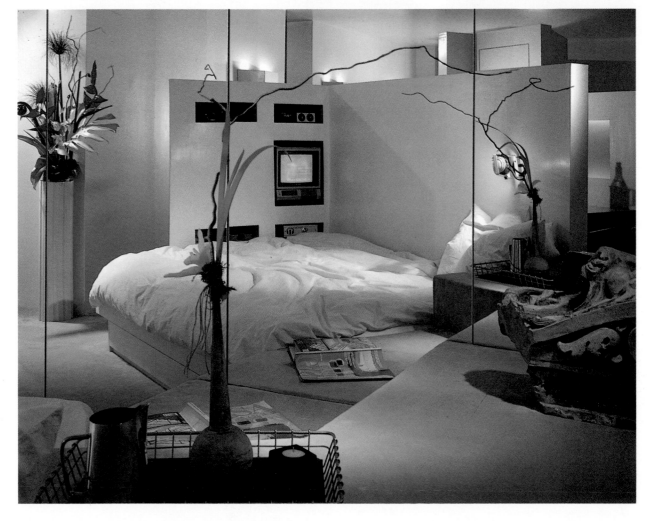

A slab of bird's-eye maple stretched between the two main dividing walls works as a desk, then as a dining table. The curved wall is squared off on this side to contain storage and a cove light which, along with small candles, animates the faces of diners. The two-corner square chairs, which push flush under the table when the space is not used, are in keeping with the smooth sculptured effects found throughout.

The bedroom is reflected in its mirrored wall. This space-extending device as well as the addition of several levels multiplies the usable surfaces. The harried urban dweller, stretched out on his comfortable bed or perched on a platform, is massaged regularly by the media.
Design: Lew Dolin
Photography: H. Durston Saylor

The open room of many functions is visually tied together by the blue-plastered ceiling, which ends on a thin brass channel that recesses into the white wall. Each room is centered on its own rug, which fits the design details that distinguish it from others. The dining area, with its thin metal-base table, Shaker-inspired chairs, zigzag brass light fixture, has a linear-pattern rug.

The living room couch with its soft cushions and stiff end-table attachments is backed by a stone triptych set into the wall. The floor throughout the living area is a warm-toned cork.

LIVING

The Co-Op

The costs of maintaining highly valued apartment houses is causing many landlords to convert their property into cooperatives. Most people who purchase shares in a building think about improving their living conditions while adding value to their already expensive piece of the sky.

The three-bedroom apartment in a New York building purchased by an architecture student is a story told every day in New York City living rooms or wherever the rumor mill grinds. The old rooms were torn down; the space was opened up to allow the solitary resident to move freely in his enormous L-shaped room. Special furnishings were designed and made.

But more than that, extraordinary care was taken by the artisans throughout: The plasterer worked like a Renaissance fresco painter to achieve the textured, mottled color. The glass artist etched the intriguing designs into the clerestory which filters light into the foyer. Another artisan did the precise sandblasting on the bottom halves of the windows, while still another made the wings of the butterfly sconces. The cabinetmaker built the many different storage units and tables, some of which jut through walls. One unit stands freely as a massive coffee table/flat file, while another attaches to the wall as a constructivist drafting table, and still another lines a wall with its strong rhythmic composition of decreasing-size drawers and openings. The carpet tufter interpreted some very delicate designs for the three rugs.

Such celebration of craftsmanship represents a new belief in tradesmen's capacity for good works, after years of their being blamed for "shoddy workmanship." All this "home improvement," needless to say, has a handsome price tag; somewhere around a quarter of a million dollars was spent.

From the living room couch through the den, which is also the drafting room and which is defined by the planar pattern of its rug, the bedroom may be seen beyond the pivoting door. Here, the large cabinet, or monumental nightstand, gives an artistic expression to the everyday function of storage.
Architecture: Steven Holl
Photography: Paul Warchol

Keeping the same horizontal dividing line which ties together all spaces in the open room, the lower parts of the windows are sandblasted for privacy. The living room's decorative theme is expressed in the solid shapes of the coffee table and the somewhat clunky couch, which is underscored by the rug's volumetric design.

LIVING
Explorations

The dynamism of modern life, often expressed in fragmented attention spans, encourages movement and exploration. There is so much to see, so much to do, so much to be a part of, and equally important, for growing numbers there's enough "disposable income" to make it all happen. The open interior, as a natural host to these new freedoms, is working its kinetic influence on the way we use furniture.

Chairs that are designed deliberately to move people through fast-food restaurants and airports are finding their way into the home. Some critics, like author Milan Kundera, call this "ugliness" but concede that it has a "positive function. No one feels like staying anywhere, people hurry on and thus arises the desirable pace of life." This pace also challenges the traditional concepts of comfort we associate with home. Furniture is often treated as art, to be looked at and valued as a unique creative expression.

In addition, the liberating influence of the room without walls has added a certain playfulness to the way we approach decoration. This may show itself in a childlike application of colors to walls and ceilings or in an uninhibited mix of refined with tacky furnishings.

In addition to the light from the veranda, the skylight, and the open passages, the living rooms of a Los Angeles house are connected to one another by a span of metal benches which were originally designed for an African airport. These benches jut through the open space into the "homey" dining area, with its wooden-trussed ceiling, which mark the change of activities. The colorful geometric fragments of the furniture are made to be noticed.
Architecture: Eric Owen Moss
Photography: Tim Street-Porter

Furniture may be built on the spot from the elements that constructed the building. In a passive solar California house, concrete blocks are assembled into artful benches, tables, and chaises that occupy the open room, where living and dining center on the recessed woodburning stove.
Architecture: Batey and Mack
Photography: Tim Street-Porter/EWA

Arrival in the living quarters of a Los Angeles house is marked by the colorful doorway and the slanted wall. Living takes shape in the room, which provides many different opportunities for relaxing—from the slim metal-framed chaise and wing chair to the tufted hotel-lobby pouf and the corner window seat. The room extends to the fenced-in garden on one side and to the dining area on the other, which has its own outdoor deck. The ubiquitous presence of television in our homes is celebrated by lifting the instrument onto an Ionic column and giving it an "antenna" of a Roman bust. The gaudily painted statue of a water maiden adds to the uninhibited fun of living.
Design: Cross/Haggerty
Photography: Tim Street-Porter

The electronically sophisticated room contains a wall of intricate hardware aligned with an ample chaise with loose pillows; a platform bed warmed by the blue light of a surreal fireplace, and a bath—all enveloped in sound. The controls for the audio/visual equipment are enclosed in a panel adjacent to the loveseat. The soft gray and black coloring and the subtle textures of the fabrics, the pleated window shades, the sculptured radiator covers, and the latticed divider wall are bathed in a tender light that is sometimes pink, then blue.
Architecture: Bromley + Jacobsen
Photography: Jaime Ardiles-Arce

LIVING
The Media Room

"I closed my eyes," remembers artist Carl Lehmann-Haupt of the time he entered another dimension in *Sound-Space,* devised in a New York loft by author Bernard Leitner. "A sound occurred," continues Lehmann-Haupt. "It was behind me, then in me, pumped into my back. It traveled through me and left me through the speaker at my feet; then traveled back again till the world around me faded away and I became involved with that one sound shuttling back and forth through my body. Thus I entered another space—sound space—shedding my rhythms and perceptions, succumbing to the rhythms of some other world."

Although such peak experiences remain the exception, the rapid develop-ments in home electronics have already changed the way many people live. Their rooms often contain prodigious amounts of attractive hardware, making whole walls look like NASA's command control center. As a result, homes are being planned for acoustics and for sound, video, computer, and software storage. These require special approaches to lighting, seating, reclining, as well as many convenient surfaces for the remote controls, the serving of foods, the sorting of magnetic tapes, laser disks, and floppy disks.

The plans must consider how much the furniture, carpeting, drapery, and objects will dampen the sound and what the residents' sound tolerances and preferences are. Considerations must be which wall or walls should be built to contain a layer of fiberglass or polyurethane soundproofing; where to place the speakers that are known to produce the best sound when they're aimed at soft or textured surfaces from an acoustically "hard" surrounding; and whether the hardware should be seen as a design element or hidden away and revealed selectively.

LIVING
The Library

Gentlemen in seventeenth-century France did it, so did New England ladies of the mid-nineteenth century, and so do media-overloaded denizens of the late twentieth century. All liked getting their information from the typeset page and the printed picture. Because of this abiding need for putting our hands on knowledge, under-lining it, writing it down, and rethinking what others have thought, the physical presence of books remains a living neces-sity for many people, even where central-ized data banks are becoming a reality.

The bookshelves which were built in nineteenth-century parlors have grown into walls of books in high-rise pent-houses, where the residents find the pres-ence of so much knowledge exhilarating and challenging. In more spacious subur-ban houses the separate library becomes the private retreat it used to be for the less harried Edwardians. Wall niches, ladders, conveniently placed tables and lamps, comfortable chairs, a fireplace, and rich wood paneling complete the romantic feeling.

Such rooms often show a new aware-ness of lighting designers' warnings against using somber-toned or dark sur-faces that have little reflectivity. The con-trast, they say, is too much: It strains the eye—the more highly strung might say the heart—suddenly to look up from the page into a muzzy room. The best lamp for reading, we're advised, should shed a good deal of light on what is now called the task, while gently illuminating the rest of the room. In addition, the seated reader is told to use an adjustable lamp or to sit so that the bottom of the lampshade is at eye level. For this advice to be practical in rooms where the lamps are somewhat tall, the light source needs to be placed be-hind the reader's shoulder.

Writers' book collections are vital to their jobs and emotional well-beings. Those who can afford it celebrate their special interests by surrounding themselves with the tools of their trade. And those whose publishers pay better than living wages often take separate rooms where they can live, privately, with their books.
The fanciful arabesque carving on the fireplace breast in this rural Pennsylvania library celebrates a writer who reads books and architecture here. Daytime work is animated by the sunlight from the tall window cut among the shelves.
Architecture: Jefferson B. Riley
Photography: Norman McGrath

A library receives the new medium of information, television, with ease in an age when generations are growing up doing homework by its electronic flicker. The peach-colored upholstery, the mushroom-toned carpet, the gray tint of the ceiling and paneling, and the light-emitting doors add enough reflectivity to the room so that the dark woods and leathers—the cliché materials of old-time libraries—are no strain on the readers' eyes.
Architecture: Gwathmey Siegel
Photography: Norman McGrath

Books in the round distinguish the living room of a Manhattan penthouse lined with warm wood surfaces, exquisite kilim rugs, and a few simple pieces of furniture and lamps.
Design: Smith and Thompson
Photography: Norman McGrath

Passionate billiard players no longer have the image of Minnesota Fats enveloped in a cloud of cigar smoke. They come in all ages, sexes, and professions. And they can play their incredible games of precision in elegant, well-lit rooms as well as in musty dives. Whether it's the Long Island sun or the recessed ceiling lights that shine on the chic cuewielders, their game is treated as a civilized pursuit of excellence.
Architecture: Gwathmey Siegel
Photography: Norman McGrath

LIVING

The Game Room

Games have played an important social role in the family since the nineteenth century when the Industrial Revolution introduced the concept of "leisure" time. These invented pastimes were meant to compete with the attractions of the greater world that drew youthful explorers away from the hearth. Gathered around the game table in the front parlor—only a few short years before serving as the scene of Bible readings—young adults were safely kept at home until the automobile. After that, though the "ideal" family was often seen glued first to the radio and then to the television, the goal of togetherness was increasingly difficult to achieve.

Now, though the younger members of the family continue to seek entertainment outside the home, youthful parents often play the games. The dread of River City (pool) and the ruin of riverboat gamblers (backgammon), as well as other once-suspect games, have been domesticated. The rooms which contain them are some of the most frequently used spaces in the home.

The perfect sound system, the play of many electronic images, and the gentle clicking of the backgammon tiles are celebrated as important activities, not just passing fancies, by their being assigned a room lined with the most expensive woods and tiles, the plushest of wool rugs, and the most luxurious leather seating ever invented.
Design: Dennis Jenkins
Photography: Steven Brooke

LIVING

The Music Room

"We must fight against the old-world house, which made a bad use of space," challenged Le Corbusier in 1921. "We must look," he went on, "upon the house as a machine for living in," and he showed in great detail the workings of interiors which were marvels of purity and restraint and almost always contained grand pianos. For decades after that, even in recent memory, magazine photographs showed spacious living rooms with grand pianos. But if for the Swiss architect the instrument was a symbol of culture, for his heirs it became a symbol of status, something to aspire to while living in mass-produced housing built by people more interested in gadgets than in music.

On the heels of what used to be called the Me Decade, people are looking for genuine self-expression. For many, the piano is an important piece of domestic furniture which can provide hours of entertainment, moments of grand illusion, achievement, and frustration. Like the book in the age of electronics, the musical instrument revives for many the special "hands-on" experience which living in machines seems to disallow.

The restrained collection of traditional and modern furniture, centered on the subdued oriental rug and attracted by the fire and the music from the upright piano, marks a new historical awareness which is firmly set in its own time.
Design: Gwen Jaffe
Photography: H. Durston Saylor

Good wine, good food, good music,
glasses sparkling in the firelight or
under the sun, and a few but choice
pieces of furniture mark the new
connoisseur. The room is simple
and functional while encouraging
civilized living.
Architecture: John Chimera
Photography: Paul Warchol

LIVING
Conversation

Rumors to the contrary, conversation is not a lost art; it merely needs to be encouraged by furnishing rooms where various persons of differing sizes and points of view can come together and turn to one another. Chairs can be moved or swiveled to express participation or separation from the issues, tilted to make a point, placed near surfaces where pipes and drinks and crumpets can be safely deposited, ringed by places where tentative participants can perch, intense companions curl up, and intimate associates stretch out, all set in the light of the sun or thoughtfully placed fixtures which expose or mystify interior vistas. These are the fresh ingredients by which civilizations are nurtured.

People are invited to change their minds and positions and form special-interest groups in tall rooms built on several levels, furnished with comfortable couches and built-in ledges. For the solitary occupant, the room is made for easy media watching, reading, telephoning, and listening to music.
Photography: Santi Caleca

Although renovations of old houses keep the spirit of separation between rooms, the new openness we seek is clearly reflected in the way we live. A small conversation pit precedes the festive dining promised beyond the partial wall.
Architecture: Booth/Hansen Assoc.
Photography: Paul Warchol

As the sun sets, voices seem to soften in response to the half-light of early evening, while the descending darkness and the distance created by the central table allow those present to drift into moments of reflection and solitude which harsher lights do not seem to tolerate in the company of others.
Photography: Santi Caleca

The light from the french doors on both sides, the crackling fire, and the glorious sound of music pull people into the tall and spacious living room through the open passages that connect the less grand areas of the house, which combines two former barns. The two different seating arrangements encourage freedom of choice.
Architecture: Shope Reno Wharton Associates
Photography: H. Durston Saylor

C H A P T E R   •   S I X

EATING

We eat more diverse foods, in more varied ways, explore more fascinating dining traditions than any generation has dreamed possible. The rapid succession of new enthusiasms is reflected in the design of homes where the traditional dining room with its bulky table and fancy centerpiece under the chandelier is only one of many options.

Space is often made for eating in rooms that are designed to be used for many different activities. Such flexible planning requires a re-thinking of storage spaces in terms of placement and use; assessing the merits of movable and foldable furniture; and choosing surfaces that stand up to the spills and scrapes that may occur each time the room is rearranged for meals as dissimilar in taste and mood as festive smorgasbords and minimal rations of raw fish.

Two daybeds with fold-up backs are pulled out from under the platform and set face-to-face across a small rug and table for cocktails. The platform hosts a sushi dinner at the low table; then the table is put away and the futon is taken out from storage and readied for sleeping.

A buffet dinner is quickly put in place as the folding tables, the movable chairs, and the benches are brought out from storage or from an adjoining room. The platform funnels traffic between the room and the balcony. Light flickers from the candles that float in the pool, the logs that burn in the fireplace, and the lamps hidden behind the silk panels that line the windows and walls.

Taking the place of the traditional china closet, the walls are used for storage space and light. On occasion one panel in the series of sliding screens is opened to reveal part of the host's impressive collections.
Architecture: Jack Lenor Larsen and Charles Forberg
Photography: Robert Grant

Cushioned benches acknowledge that seats for eating need not be restricted to the positions allowed by upright chairs.

The Open Plan

Rooms without walls, arranged so there's lots of space to move about and deposit things on conveniently placed surfaces, encourage casual and impromptu gatherings. Instead of having to move the furniture to fit the occasion, it's simply a question of finding and settling into the spot that fits the needs and mood of the moment and the person.

Hibiscus tea by the fireplace, fettucine brought steaming from the open kitchen and served to a large gathering at the official dining table, omelets made for a quick supper in the kitchen and kebabs roasted on the hibachi grill on the deck may be separate individual occasions or combine an evening of entertainments where friends feel free to settle into the manner of eating that suits them.

The small lightweight table on the glassed-in porch that connects the interior to the exterior sets a sunny mood for quick breakfasts or during drawn-out Sunday brunches that may meander out to the flower-lined deck.
Architecture: Hank Koning and Julie Eizenberg
Photography: Tim Street-Porter

The large table, placed by the partial wall that connects to the kitchen, holds food for a formal dinner. Its proximity to the bookshelves, which can be closed off by a sliding door, also makes it a much-used work surface.

A small, square table, set among plush sitting pieces, hosts a solitary writer, a pair of game players, a casual group of snackers, or an intimate company of diners.
Design: John Saladino
Photography: Peter Vitale

Open to the light from the surrounding rooms during the day, the library, set on an oriental rug, is used as a workroom with space enough to spread out. At night, the doors are shut, and the dark green walls and wooden shelves play in mysterious shadows by the flicker of the candle flames reflected in the mirrored bar.
Design: Gwen Jaffe
Photography: H. Durston Saylor

EATING

The Change-Over

Eating is often just one of the many activities that take place in the dining area. A large table in a well-lit space will be useful for balancing checkbooks, doing taxes, cutting patterns and other tasks. These uses are often discovered accidentally by a family member looking for a place to spread out. But areas can be planned to ensure that maximum use is made of each room. A table placed in a hallway may be a deposit for letters and packages, then converted to dining as the stacking or folding chairs are brought out. A library with its central table may serve a home business during the day and transform to a room in which elegant dinners are served.

EATING

The Formal Dinner

The latin root of the word company is *cum pane*. And breaking bread with others continues to be one of life's chief delights.

The banquet, that traditional celebration from medieval times, when long trestle tables stretched across drafty halls and diners were served by an army of footmen, requires a grand scale. Most dining, however, is a simple affair of smaller dimensions where the arts of more personal hospitality are displayed.

The experience of sitting at a dining table reflects attitudes about food, time, and people. The distances between persons as well as furniture styles express these. The setting of the table, the placing of the chairs, and their relative comfort, indicate what the evening will provide. A glass-top table calls attention to shoes, ankles, and knees that are best kept out of sight if people are self-conscious. Stiff chairs encourage quick eating while comfortable seats allow leisurely conversations to progress through many different courses.

Three tables line up for a ceremonious meal, candle flames glow in eyes and on crystal and silver. The slim torchère lamp in the corner washes the ceiling with a gentle light.
Photography: Santi Caleca

The seat of honor, at either end of the shimmering table, is given unusual distinction by the two chintz-covered wing chairs.
Architecture: Muller and Murphy
Photography: Michael Dunne/EWA

The generous dining table in a renovated Italian farmhouse is charmingly surrounded by diverse wooden chairs.
Design: Teresa Pomodoro and Giancarlo Montebelle
Photography: Antonio Mulas/ Abitare

In a Mexican house of many white-walled rooms there is a festive pink-painted enclosure which contains a large unvarnished table and built-in counters made of the native sabeño wood, known for its silky surface. There are no hanging lamps, which age faces by casting shadows under their eyes, only a simple parchment-shaded lamp on the large serving credenza.
Architecture: Luis Barragán
Photography: Allen Carter

The translucency of glass is preserved without its revealing transparency by the tabletop made from three layers of differently textured glass, which combine into a unique surface pattern. The metal table is cantilevered from the wall with its black glass inset that picks up highlights of people and objects. The chairs with their short, rounded arms, originally designed for a Viennese cafe at the beginning of this century, encourage sitting sideways as conversations carry on through coffee.
Design: Kevin Walz
Photography: Peter Vitale

The metal mesh chairs are molded
to the contours of the body.
Recessed ceiling fixtures, wall
sconces, a hanging lamp, and
candles can create different moods
in a variety of combinations.
Architecture: Leslie Armstrong
Photography: Norman McGrath

The traditional chandelier is a
highly decorative addition to a
room that makes a virtue of abstract
design and minimal furnishings. The
relief-sculptured wall and the
unique dining set, with its stiff
chairs, fill the room with
contradictions about "dining
comfort."
Architecture: Calvin Tsao
Photography: Paul Warchol

Whether it's breakfast or dinner, the translucent fabric tent adds a romantic glow to a meal.

EATING
Al Fresco

The garden with its perfumed scents, peaceful sounds, shimmering leaves, changing colors, and cool pools of water is a sensuous backdrop for a meal. This may be a Sunday brunch served at a small table, midday refreshments brought to a bench in the shade, a covered space that keeps out flying insects but lets in the cool breezes, as well as other ways of bringing people and food close to the nature that made them both, adding a special meaning to the everyday need for nourishment.

A small table overlooking the garden is warmed by the sun in all seasons. The tent, shaped like an African hut, stands near the trellised arbor.
Design: Jack Lenor Larsen
Photography: Paul Warchol

A shady poolside is perfect for a light luncheon served in ceramic bowls.
Design: Jack Lenor Larsen
Photography: Paul Warchol

Elegant crystal, silver, and china are brought out and arranged artfully on a lush linen tablecloth by the pool.
Design: Steven Farrish
Photography: Peter Vitale

A small fountain funnels waters into a lighted pool and adds to the pleasures of one backyard in the urban wilderness.
Architecture: Goshow Assoc.
Photography: Derrick and Love

This thicket of backwoods is manicured near the house, where the landscaping adds the sound of a fountain and provides plenty of room for garden chairs.
Architecture: Harry Williams
Photography: Norman McGrath

In the land of the midnight sun summer is a joyous occasion filled with outdoor activities. Picnics are quickly set up on the grass lawns, on blankets, pillows, lounge chairs, under parasols.
Architecture: Antti Nurmesniemi

Sea breezes from the coral reefs cool the air under a protective trellis roof.
Design: Doris LaPorte
Photography: Paul Warchol

Cultivating a small garden on a confined city deck has the reward of taking food under the sun.
Design: Jeremy Linden
Photography: Michael Nicholson/
EWA

CHAPTER • SEVEN

WORKING

Home is where the work is for persons charged with the care and feeding of the household. While each room requires constant maintenance, it is in the kitchen that domestic work has been studied most successfully. Body motions involved in cooking, serving, and washing up have been analyzed by every new profession, from engineering to psychology, since mechanization began to take command. The result is the many labor saving appliances which continue to promise to cut house work to a minimum.

There are refrigerators with ice makers, frost-free freezers, self-cleaning ovens, microwave ovens with browning capabilities, dishwashers with pot-scrubbing and crystal cycles, and washers made to clean the many new fibers woven into clothing. In addition, a growing number of gadgets and attachments are designed to make anything from pasta to cappuccino to gelato.

The kitchen, as the mechanical heart of the house, is also attracting other work. The small office with its files and typewriter is fitted conveniently into the cabinetry which also adapts to the home computer. This new machine brings the work of budgeting, preparing taxes, tallying calories, and keeping shopping lists and inventories to the room where the hidden electrical current is the last vestige of the hearth.

The many-angled center island may encourage visitors to participate in the preparation of the meal. The built-in shelving along the walls includes a small desktop with reference materials at easy reach and an open counter for serving.
Architecture: Gerald Kagan
Photography: Robert Perron

The California sun lights the preparation of food and its consumption through a skylight cut over the central island sink area and clerestory windows over the corner table. Plentiful storage is mostly hidden behind the plywood cabinet doors, which are in material and aesthetic agreement with the exposed wood structure of the room.
Architecture: Frank O. Gehry
Photography: Tim Street-Porter

WORKING
The Kitchen

Tasks performed in the kitchen are most frequently organized around a work triangle, at each tip of which is located a major appliance. Thus, the refrigerator is placed adjacent to the surfaces where food preparation takes place, surrounded by storage for frequently used utensils; the range is conveniently near the storage for pots and pans and spices, as well as surfaces where the progress of cooking foods may be inspected; the sink and dishwasher best serve the jobs of food preparation and cleaning up where there are places to

Appliances and storage hug the walls of the cooking area, which is open to the surrounding living area. Several options for eating are provided: perching at a snack bar; informal sitting at the table; or a more formal dining in the alcove of the greenhouse.
Design: Shelly and Janet Rosenberg
Photography: H. Durston Saylor

stack things and nearby storage for them.

Although there are scientifically tested dimensions for each area, such as the recommended four- to seven-foot counterspace between the sink and the refrigerator, the household's eating habits provide the real clues to kitchen planning. Minimal cooking, for instance, requires plentiful storage for convenience foods and efficient warming appliances. Elaborate foods made from fresh ingredients dictate a plan with plentiful counterspace, extra sinks and electrical outlets for small appliances, as well as precision instruments.

Although there are as many approaches to food preparation as there are kitchens, the universal need to be with others continues to influence kitchen design. This may show up as a separate table, a padded nook, or a minimal counter.

The seamless room encourages thinking about how we want to live. In houses where entertaining is important, the kitchen is the natural adjunct to the living space. Its open counters encourage sociability. Instead of treating food preparation as a secret alchemy that must be carried on in its segregated space, the open room invites everyone to share in the work and pleasures of nurturing.

The idea of cooking companions is not a new one. It was briefly forgotten when industrial societies specialized everything, from factory assembly lines to rooms in the house. In the search for "efficiencies," the applied sciences filled the woman's workroom—the kitchen— with "laborsaving" gadgets and turned her into a solitary worker, whose job as a cook was largely devalued by the many new "convenience foods." The desire for openness, then, is as much a sign of the need to break away from outworn specializations as the new interest in fresh foods.

Located along the wall of glass, which communes freely with the outside, the instruments of cooking, washing up, and storing are given direct access to an elegant sitting area distinguished by the most prestigious designs for twentieth-century living: Le Corbusier's 1928 pony-skin sling chair, a pair of Miës van der Rohe's chairs and his chrome and glass table from the 1930s, a ubiquitous modern cube and modular lounge seating, all centered on a colorful handmade kilim rug.
Architecture: David Hovey
Photography: © Bill Hedrich/
Hedrich-Blessing

In a renovation that opened up the rooms of a nineteenth-century Milan town house, the kitchen was kept separate but easily accessible to the adjacent dining room. Food is prepared and dishes are cleaned in the narrow room with its appliances and undercounter storage for things needed nearby. The slim-profile translucent mesh-glass fume hood with its metal frame keeps the room from looking crowded. The open passage to the cooking area on one side is marked by reminders of the building's history: a small inset window and the old fireplace. On the other side there's a partial access to the dining room through the serving counter with its sinktop. The dining room is simply furnished by a square wooden table with a laminate top and open shelving made of the same light wood. The delicate hanging lamps are positioned to shed light on each activity, yet preserve the great openness of the space.
Architecture: Carlo Santi
Photography: Gabriele Basilico/ Abitare

The owners of a small Connecticut house built in the 1920s wanted to combine a kitchen with dining and family rooms in one space with an option to close off the work area from the rest. Cooking is accommodated by handsome cabinetwork with tiled work tops. Storage is zoned to each area of activity. From the variously sized shallow shelves behind glass doors it's possible to retrieve the right spice and the appropriate table setting without rummaging among layers of items. Sliding doors separate the adjoining room on two sides.
Architecture: Shope Reno Wharton Associates
Photography: H. Durston Saylor

The old picture window over the sink becomes a wall that lights the entire span of the kitchen where attractive white surfaces are Complemented by the strong red of the overhead beams, the wooden table, and an occasional bright appliance taken from the plentiful storage walls, the continuous work surface that runs along the glass wall is equipped with a desk area and files. The workroom blends into the adjacent dining room beyond the open serving counter.
Architecture: David Hovey
Photography: ©Bill Hedrich/ Hedrich-Blessing

The modern work triangle—cold storage at one tip, heat source at another, and water at the third—fits easily into a traditional design recalled in the exquisite woodwork of the cabinetry, the ornamental moldings, dado, and columns, the borders inlaid on the floor, a bench shaped to the window niche, and the round table.
Architecture: Peter Gisolfi
Photography: Norman McGrath

An operating table is made into a serving cart and additional work surface that easily travels between the kitchen and its adjoining areas.
Design: Ward Bennett
Photography: Norman McGrath

A table shaped to fit the area of the cushioned window seat adds an attractive work surface to the long wooden plank of the counter.
Architecture: Ken Walker
Photography: Mark Ross

A curved counter extends a small kitchen's work surfaces and makes room for quick meals.
Architecture: Reale-Frojd
Photography: Paul Warchol

A favorite place in many houses, for shelling peas, talking on the phone, or doing homework, is the breakfast nook. This 1950s style corner revives some sweet memories of ice cream parlors with their pink banquettes and layered cake displays.
Design: Kim Milligan
Photography: Tim Street-Porter

Two open shelves carry a neat line-up of favorite spices near the countertop used for mixing foods; cooking utensils hang from the bottom of the third shelf, which is placed over the range. A clip-on lamp is centered on each work area.
Architecture: Yolanda Collamanti Wiskemann
Photography: Gabriele Basilico/ Abitare

Counter space is stretched by the use of the smooth-surface cooktop and the second sink, which is served by a chopping block/storage cube. The elegant joinings of the woodwork, the tall layers of windows, and the lamps suspended over each work area add to the joy of cooking.
Architecture: Jefferson B. Riley
Photography: Norman McGrath

Work areas are served by the two sinks and expanded by the stepped-back design of the cabinets. Favorite items for cooking and serving are easily found behind glass.
Architecture: Leslie Armstrong
Photography: Norman McGrath

In addition to the expected window over the sink, which looks into the backyard, the pleasant glow from the sky, and the surprising wedge under the roofline, there are small windows which frame fragments of views and provide ventilation. One is niched into the corrugated plastic cabinet while two are placed near the range.
Architecture: Eric Owen Moss
Photography: Tim Street-Porter

Minimal cooking is served by small-scale appliances which leave room for a worktop, a band of sockets under the hanging cabinet for small gadgets, and a neat place to store them.
Architecture: Peter Marino
Photography: Norman McGrath

An extensive collection of phonograph records, which need complicated shelving for storage and display, may seem a bulky alternative to the miniaturized record-keeping capabilities of the home computer. But for the present this new tool helps organize, code, and retrieve instantaneously any item on the list.
Photography: Morley von Sternberg

The office in the attic contains the standard furnishings found in the "rabbit warrens" at corporate headquarters—the metal files, the boxy desk, and the task light. The sun and views all around and the padded niche between the reference bookshelves make working a pleasurable pursuit.
Architecture: Charles Jencks and Buzz Yudell
Photography: Tim Street-Porter

WORKING
The Studio

Work is no longer given the narrow definition of something a person does for a wage outside the home. Some people commute from bedroom to living room in their robes and work at all hours. Others regularly start their days in basements, garages, attics, kitchens, or wherever their tools may be set up. Many are already living in "electronic cottages," at a time when the new technologies have added the option of working at home to other alternatives.

The more leisurely pace generally associated with the private world of home is reflected in the arrangement and appearance of the workroom. Places to lie down and wander about may be seen as time wasters by some, but help relax and refresh both body and mind for the next stretch of concentrated work.

The ordered clutter of a writer's desktop puts current reference materials within reach, while future topics are filed in many small drawers lined up under the window.
Design: Dorit Egli
Photography: Michael Nicholson/ EWA

A small double shelf, niched into the decorative woodwork of the room surrounded by favorite objects, is ideal for written correspondence.
Design: Lorenzo Berni and Alberto Grimoldi
Photography: Santi Caleca

A desk, a lamp, a phone, a chair may be enough to do the job, but the easy access to references, the bella vista, the space to move about and out, the changing colors and textures, and an easy chair for curling up or stretching out—all show an understanding of the active body and the searching mind at work.
Architecture: Harry Williams
Photography: Norman McGrath

"A design must be contemporary, yet with the capacity to survive," says Cleto Munari, producer of a wide range of domestic objects designed by architects. In his Vicenza, Italy, home, where he has lived since childhood, his office contains a pleasant assortment of survivors, like Arne Jacobsen's chairs and Marcel Breuer's chaise, which look comfortable in the company of the Sharp computer.
Photography: Santi Caleca

The floors, the walls, the tables, the deck outside and the pool are all used for working, which for artist David Hockney means seeing always new details in the rooms he made for himself and including them in his illusionistic paintings.
Photography: Tim Street-Porter

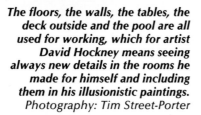

The windows are used as a backlight on the drafting table, where the work at hand is illuminated by the lamps that also adjust to reading on the couch.
Architecture: Calvin Tsao
Photography: Paul Warchol

The wild flowers an artist transplants around his house in the Michigan dunes show up in such works as the painting of "Cattails and Cardinal Flowers," which hangs in the northern light of the studio, separate from the main house. The artist's practical needs, such as balanced light, places to mix paints and wash out brushes, and moments to sit back and look over what was made, are accommodated with simplicity.
Architecture: Veronda Associates
Photography: © Bill Hedrich/
Hedrich-Blessing

CHAPTER • EIGHT

WORKING OUT

The human body is made for movement. Yet at every step there's someone figuring out how to decrease motion, make it more efficient and less strenuous. That someone may be the lone jogger thinking up step-saving plans for kitchens in which everything is reached without stretching, bending, stooping, or much walking about. These natural movements of everyday living, then, are summarily reduced to mere finger exercises.

Keeping the modern muscle lean and hard has become a booming industry. All sorts of mechanical devices are made to push, pull, and knead every forgotten tissue. At home some of these racks, benches, bars, ropes, and pulleys are showing up in basements and bedrooms as well as in specifically designed rooms of their own for thoroughgoing workouts.

Away from the sedentary pursuit of creative drawing at the drafting tables, which also occupy this open New York loft, coordination of another kind is tested on the rings which hang in the middle of the spacious living area.
Architecture: Peix and Crawford
Photography: Tim Street-Porter

The results of workouts on the machines or at the bar are critically inspected in the mirrored wall under bright lights.
Design: Engel Yorkley Associated
Photography: Derrick and Love

A Swedish exercise ladder on the bedroom wall is used for a morning stretch or to hang clothing worn that day.
Design: Piero Polato
Photography: Paola Mattioli/ Abitare

The glassed-in pool, which can be opened up to the outside on warm days, encourages frequent exercise through the seasons.
Architecture: Wilkes and Faulkner
Photography: Norman McGrath

WORKING OUT
The Pool

Our need for daily regeneration has been understood since the Greeks established their gymnasia. Here the life of the body and the life of the mind were fused in a setting that encouraged strong physical effort, followed by cold showers and other ablutions, which alerted the mind to challenging discourse and contemplation. We come close to combining these experiences in the space designed for the swimming pool and its surroundings.

The protective overhangs, which shade the house from the strong Mexican sun, have been extended to cover part of the swimming pool. The lava stone decking gives traction to wet feet.
Architecture: Luis Barragán
Photography: Allen Carter

Added to a fifty-year-old Dutch Colonial-style house, the indoor pool is made for a Connecticut family committed to daily exercise. Its shallow waters (four feet deep) are sufficient for swimming while allowing its occupants to take advantage of the attractively framed views. Necessary precautions to isolate the heat and humidity generated by the room have been taken to protect the adjoining house.
Architecture: Shope Reno Wharton Associates
Photography: H. Durston Saylor

Society gathers for the seasonal
pleasure of swimming in
Connecticut. The pool—newly
added to one of only three houses
built in America by the father of
International Style architecture,
Ludwig Miës van der Rohe—has
direct access to the interior showers
and bath.
Architecture: Peter Gluck
Photography: Paul Warchol

The tented loggia and the adjoining
pool front encourage cool social
gatherings in tropical Coconut
Grove, Florida, while the blue
waters invite swimmers.
Architecture: Andres Duany and
Elizabeth Plater-Zyberk
Photography: Steven Brooke

The lush plant life of South Florida
is allowed, within reason, to invade
the pool area, which is furnished
with sturdy chairs and chaises, and
connected to an open room under
the roof overhang.
Architecture: Barry Sugarman and
E.D. Stone, Jr.
Photography: Steven Brooke

The Spa

A modern alternative to the massage is often called the spa. This may refer to a hot tub, which is actually a large, round barrel made of redwood or cedar planks, or to a whirlpool, which is a tub molded in many sizes and shapes from the more yielding materials of metal, acrylic, and fiberglass. These containers are made to submerge the body in four feet of heated water, which is vibrated by strategically angled hydrojets that pound the flesh with either forceful or gentle thrusts.

Additions to a former Los Angeles tract house and its garage connect the swimming pool and the whirlpool bath by a series of vertical passages. The guesthouse/ studio has rope-railed stairs swinging down to poolside, from which the fire escape climbs up the back of the main house. Here, on the rooftop, whirlpool bathers are treated to a view of the Santa Monica Freeway, Century City, and the Mormon Temple.
Architecture: Eric Owen Moss
Photography: Tim Street-Porter

Celebrating Los Angeles's trend-setting reputation, the house in Rustic Canyon gathers a collection of stylishly post modern buildings around a California-shaped swimming pool and the pavilion-shaded hot tub, both of which light up at night.
Architecture: Charles Jencks, Buzz Yudell, Charles Moore
Photography: Tim Street-Porter

A skylit room with large windows, good ventilation, and tile floors with drainage is made for year-round whirlpool bathing in northern climates.
Architecture: Marsden Moran and Andrew Robinson
Photography: Karen Bussolini

Physical exertion around a New England solar house is relieved in the sun space, which integrates a comfortable sitting area at one end with a hot tub at the other.
Architecture: Don Metz
Photography: Robert Perron

Outdoor whirlpool bathers are guarded against wind chill by reed screens and against sunburn by the trellised overhang.
Courtesy of Lynda Gaynor and Fred Bennett
Photography: Karen Bussolini

WORKING OUT
The Sauna

A traditional sauna, with its woodburning cast-iron stove, raw pine paneling, tiny (double-glazed) window with a lamp between the panes for night light, is the back room of a small cabin that faces the sunset and a lake in the Stockholm archipelago. The front room, with its cot, shelves, storage cabinets and hooks, and open hearth, is the resting place for weekend skiers, skaters, sailors, and hikers.
Architecture: Bernt Sahlin
Photography: Lars Hallén

It's the spirit, say the Finns, that rises from the fiery stones of the sauna when a few drops of water are sprinkled on them to add moisture to the dry, hot rooms many continue to build for the regeneration of the body. In these raw pine cabins with hard benches layered on several levels to take advantage of the rising heat, intense perspiration is provoked by temperatures of up to 100°C. A handful of birch twigs, used to whip the flesh to stimulate the circulation, adds its fragrance to the room's scent of pungent smoked woods. A quick tumble in the snow or a splash in the brisk lake waters completes the process of purification that began in silence, seclusion, and semidarkness.

In the basement of a Helsinki house the traditional Finnish sauna is updated with an electric stove, an adjoining room for the cold shower, and a dressing room, where towels and robes are stored in heated closets.
Architecture: Ilkka Salo
Photography: Lars Hallén

CHAPTER • NINE

CLEANSING

The modern bather is both the beneficiary and the victim of plumbing efficiencies. The economic need to consolidate the three, sometimes four, standard fixtures in one small room has given us the water closet. Aptly named, it's planned for the swift routines of cleansing the body of its surface and interior wastes. It does this admirably well when people function like clockwork and schedules settle into routines. In less disciplined households the bathroom is the battleground of opposing forces, which calls attention to the flaws in the planning. The most frequently used solution is the addition of another such room, which successfully separates people instead of bodily functions.

Aside from its water-carrying capabilities, the toilet has no real reason to be in the same room as the bathtub. The Japanese understood this very well, although they, too, are becoming victims of plumbing. Their traditions were built on the natural division between the private toilet and the communal bath, which, in turn, made a clear distinction between the acts of washing and bathing. Not for them was the barbarian custom of solitary soaking in waters filmed with oils, soap suds, fragments of skin, and hair.

Provision for brief sitting is made by the small wooden bench in the glass-enclosed shower.
Design: John Saladino
Photography: Peter Vitale

Washing in the shower before sinking into the soaking tub is made possible by two adjacent fixtures. One of the two mirrors of the dressing table encourages close inspection of makeup while seated in front of its magnifying glass.
Architecture: Gwathmey Siegel
Photography: Norman McGrath

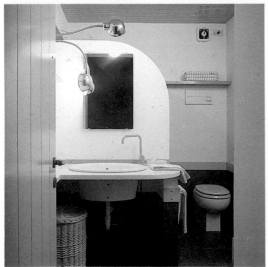

A curved wall separates quick washing up from the more thorough task of bathing. An open shelf keeps extra towels at the ready.
Architecture: Yolanda Collamanti Wiskemann
Photography: Gabriele Basilico/ Abitare

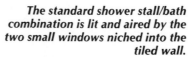

The standard shower stall/bath combination is lit and aired by the two small windows niched into the tiled wall.
Architecture: Eric Owen Moss
Photography: Tim Street-Porter

ı wo people running to catch the same commuter train are kept out of each other's way in the washroom by a double set of fixtures. The shower is at one end, the bath at the other, while two sinks give plenty of elbowroom; toilets and bidets are separated by a partial wall, and large mirrors hang on opposing walls. The border design of the floor tile underscores the territorial divisions.
Architecture: Carlo Santi
Photography: Gabriele Basilico/
Abitare

Privacy is sacrificed for the sake of openness. The shower is placed in a transparent bubble, the toilet, bidet and sink are clustered at the center; and accessories and towels stored on glass and chrome racks.
Design: Doris LaPorte
Photography: Paul Warchol

The whirlpool tub, built into the travertine wall under the window, has a view of the garden and the sky. The room is ventilated by high windows and ceiling fans.
Architecture: Batey and Mack
Photography: Tim Street-Porter

The mirrored wall ends at the tiled partition that protects the privacy of the shower.
Design: Dennis Jenkins
Photography: Steven Brooke

Balmy Balinese breezes are invited into the bath, which communes with nature from the protected enclosure of a private courtyard.
Architecture: Henk Vos
Photography: Tim Street-Porter

A small bathroom that squeezes shower and bath into one compact corner is decorated by the ornamental plasterwork, the light from above, and the old-fashioned hardware.
Design: Carl D'Aquino
Photography: Paul Warchol

C H A P T E R • T E N

RESTING

The body at rest requires support, warmth, quiet, and the feeling of security. These may be provided anyplace there is room to stretch out, away from the traffic of the household. A protected corner or a darkened room or a piece of sky make it possible to retreat into a kind of refreshing solitude that Thomas Merton called a "deepening of the present."

The bed, because it is designed for the prolonged resting that takes place between falling asleep and rising, needs to provide more than bodily comfort. Its placement can become a personal expression of how we like to start and end the day. Some prefer darkness at both the point of retreat and re-entry. Others like to make a clear distinction between the two by waking, without mechanical alarms, to the sun's intensifying light.

The marriage bed used to be the place where most people were born and died. Because of this, it was a potent symbol of the lifecycle that had a definite beginning and end, reinforced each day by the new light of morning and the dark of night. Now that our entry and exit into the world have been given over to high technology, the bed's old ceremonial function is largely lost. It has become a luxuriously padded scaffold which supports our escapes into the dreamworlds of television and the mysteries of our uneasy unconscious.

Richly detailed roof overhangs guard the coolness of the tropical interior's tile-clad bedroom, where a rosy mist filters through the pink cotton fabric that hangs from the ceiling.
Architecture: Henk Vos
Photography: Tim Street-Porter

Morning light pours through the glass wall of the resident artist's spacious bedroom. When he wants to sleep late or there are guests staying across the meadow in his studio, he stretches a tangle of blue fabric across the glass for a slower penetration of light.
Architecture: Veronda Associates
Photography: © Bill Hedrich/ Hedrich-Blessing

Light from across the window seat with its invitingly padded perch is filtered for sleeping late by the crisp curtains which pull around the bed.
Design: Jack Lenor Larsen
Photography: Paul Warchol

Open to the stairwell and the woods beyond the glass wall, the bedroom's privacy may be protected by pulling the accordion door shut. Wardrobes built into the opposing walls contain recessed dressing mirrors: stand-up for him, sit-down for her.
Architecture: Harry Williams
Photography: Norman McGrath

Waking to the morning sun is aided by dormer windows of various sizes and shapes in upstairs rooms for residents and guests.
Architecture: Graham Gund Assoc.
Photography: Steve Rosenthal

In this master bedroom the impressive columns, drapery, and trellised headboard extend the dimensions of the mattress. In the guest room the delicate Gothic motif of the bed frame echoes "Melancholy," David Remfrey's painting over the desk.
Architecture: Charles Jencks and Buzz Yudell
Photography: Tim Street-Porter

The mattress, simply placed on the floor under the skylight, needs to be turned and rotated occasionally to avoid condensation of moisture underneath.
Design: Cross/Haggarty
Photography: Tim Street-Porter

The 1950s inspiration of this bedroom does not extend to the television, its VCR and computer attachments, which are treated as pieces of furniture in their own right.
Design: Kim Milligan
Photography: Tim Street-Porter

A row of three closets separates the sleeping area from the rest of the bedroom while allowing the light to pass between and over them.
Photography: Hank Konig and Julie Eizenberg
Photography: Tim Street-Porter

The bed's frame and springing are made of natural pine strips which extend out from both sides of the headboard as bedside tables.
Architecture: Carlo Santi
Photography: Gabriele Basilico/ Abitare

The sitting area with its fireplace, plush chairs and polar-bear hearth rug is separated from the sleeping area by the low shelving unit, into which the bed is niched.
Architecture: Gwathmey Siegel
Photography: Norman McGrath,
Paul Warchol

Peaceful rest on an ample platform bed with a wide black ledge for safely placing things is "menaced" by tumbling foam rocks and the falling architectural fragments screen-printed on the gray flannel fabric.
Design: Paul Fortune
Photography: Tim Street-Porter

RESTING

The Greenhouse

When the canopy of leaves—so protective of the house during the summer's heat—is gone from the surrounding trees the big sky opens up and the landscape becomes hard-edged and linear. Then a solarium, added to an old clapboard house, acts as a soft cushion of warmth, where people, plants, and pets are nurtured by the light of the sun.

Basking in this glow—even if for a moment of passing through or during drawn-out Sunday brunches served from the adjacent kitchen or while working to maintain the lush plant life—is made more pleasant and economically prudent by the use of double- or triple-glazed windows and roofs, which cut down the heat loss. Tiles, made from the earth's own material, also trap the warmth and radiate it to the living things within.

The entry from the deck to the kitchen becomes a moment to treasure in the lively solarium, which separates the outside and the inside yet brings the two together.

Glass shelves underscore the rare and delicate flowers grown here without obstructing the transparency of the space. For the more hardy strains of plant life, the low wooden ledge has been installed over the radiator. Moments of rest in between activities are encouraged by comfortable chairs and places on which to put cups, books, and work tools.
Architecture: Peter Gisolfi
Photography: Norman McGrath

RESTING
The Niche

While some architects continue to favor the vast scenes that present themselves through wide ribbons of glass, others like to work on a series of smaller canvases. Their windows cut up views into more intimate pictures which become unique additions to each room. To be inside such houses is to be treated to many different experiences, where moving from room to room is a series of close encounters with the surrounding world. These encourage a slowing of pace and lingering and finding the favorite spot of the moment.

Small light-filled areas around windows invite dreamers, readers, and loungers. A niche, warmed, lighted, and textured by a fireplace and a captivating view, pushes the interior space outward and claims a small part of the greater world, as does a window seat with its inviting cushions. Rooms so connected to the outside, though they may be small in measure, can feel generous to the person enclosed within.

A separate little room is made in a niche where a window provides an ever-changing picture of the sea. The light can be controlled by a simple roll-up shade on the arched glass and by old-fashioned shutters.

Whether it is used as a daytime perch for dreaming or as a nighttime lounge for reading by the recessed light, this window seat adds a special texture to the bedroom by extending it beyond the walls which limit it.

A freestanding wall, its small and large windows framing the views from the porch and the adjacent dining room, is a playful addition to the many different views from this house on Long Island Sound (see page 18).
Architecture: Graham Gund Assoc.
Photography: Steve Rosenthal

RESTING
The Ledge

Escaping from the interior enclosure, no matter how pleasant this may be, is an emotional and physical necessity for residents of small urban apartments as well as for those in large suburban houses. A balcony, a deck, a porch underscore these moments of freedom. These extensions of the interior change the scale, alter the atmospheric conditions, and introduce new sounds and scents while they remain secure places associated with the inside.

Here, in the world in between, are created powerful perceptions of control over vast spaces, where lofty thoughts and great expectations are encouraged. City dwellers talk of getting a "high" as they step onto a balcony, eyes scanning the skyline, minds rushing to identify landmarks and to imagine the activities of other people behind the many windows. Some can even hear the birds above the city's insistent mechanical hum.

In the country the deck, shaded and protected, gives an immediacy, a reality to the natural world that goes about its eternal business often unnoticed. The scent of petunias, the sounds of nesting birds, the moon showing itself are reassuring companions for resting.

In the Michigan dunes, surrounded by wild grasses and flowers which the artist who lives and works here has carefully transplanted to grow a thicket, the deck, with its wooden trellis and steel wall, is an emphatic moment which brings man's work together with nature's own creations.
Architecture: Veronda Associates
Photography: © Bill Hedrich/ Hedrich-Blessing

An arched door to a balcony which opens to the built wonders of Milan marks the transition between the small enclosure of the apartment and the open city.
Design: Lorenzo Berni and Alberto Grimoldi
Photography: Santi Caleca

RESTING

The Courtyard

Instead of opening up vast spaces, the courtyard encloses a small area and pulls it into the house. It provides opportunities for communing with nature on a manageable and private scale. It claims part of the sky for the house, putting the tenants of one in touch with the tenants of the other: people watching passing clouds and migratory birds and perhaps the reverse.

The world beyond the high walls is a mystery, a cause for speculation and intrigue, for both those within and those without.

High, strong walls, almost like those of Aztec temples, offer places for contemplating the world in the solitude of Mexican courtyards. With places to sit and spaces to wander under the shading trees, these intensely private enclosures become generous containers of lively fiestas.

A small courtyard, within a larger one, encloses a brimming pool of water that reflects, like a living mirror, the sky and brings its light and texture into the house through the adjacent window.
Architecture: Luis Barragán
Photography: Allen Carter

RESTING
The Garden

Nowadays, when designers talk about humanizing the environment, they often say it with flowers and plants. They enthusiastically install giant ficuses and bamboo groves in city apartments, which require the invention of ingenious techniques to keep the residents in touch with nature.

In the tropics the reverse is true. The lush vegetation naturally moves in on the house, bringing with it a cacophony of sounds, scents, textures, and colors; "humanizing" here means cutting through the brush to make space for people. Under such conditions the environment insists on becoming an integral part of the house with its open passages around rooms, garden paths which lead to covered rest stops, and a magnificent variety of flora everywhere.

A Balinese garden is made into a spot of home by a thatched open room which elegantly combines the fanciful styles of native Hinduism and the crispness of Dutch colonial heritages.

The tiled veranda, which shelters the interior rooms of the house, is patterned by a canopy of native teakwood and singing birds in cages.
Architecture: Henk Vos
Photography: Tim Street-Porter

CHAPTER ELEVEN

GROWING UP

A chance visitor to Charlotte Perkins Gilman's *Herland* observes that "houses and gardens for babies had in them nothing to hurt—no stairs, no corners, no small objects to swallow, no fire...." Houses in "ourland," instead, are made for adults. Children get a set of operating instructions that are supposed to take them safely through their volatile growing-up years. Even in their own rooms—meant to teach them about privacy, independence, and responsibility for their surroundings—they confront adult fantasies and aspirations. These may show up in such lovingly planned fictions as frilly bassinets, over-designed castle beds, and work stations for junior computers. Each plan comes with its own set of behavioral expectations.

But the freedom to maneuver and to change things is important to everyone and essential for children. Rooms designed too specifically for one stage of development confine the next stage. Conversely, designers of rooms that provide opportunities for things to happen recognize, as Frank Lloyd Wright did, that a "child...is a beginning."

The brief months when a tiny infant needs a cozy container may be well served by such household items as a securely padded drawer, a wicker basket or its more formal version, the bassinet.
Photography: Jerry Tubby/EWA

Plenty of room is left for maneuvering tiny cars or bulkier playthings along the carpeted floors, on the window ledge, and even under the bed, which combines function with fantasy.
Architecture: Calvin Tsao
Photography: Paul Warchol

The special needs for bodily protection and maintenance, during what seems like a moment between early infancy and toddlerhood, require the safety of adjustable cribs as well as conveniently-placed dressing tables with accessible storage spaces. Things to look at and tell stories about amuse both the caretaker and the naturally inquisitive offspring.
Photography: Yolande Flesch

Youthful dreamers who live in apartment houses may know about attics only from the stories they read, but they continue to be attracted to high perches. The bed, raised on a storage cabinet, adds the experience of level change to a room that encourages the freedoms to lounge and change places from the soft floor to the couch to the cushions to the steps.
Design: Gwen Jaffe
Photography: H. Durston Saylor

No crowded, slippery-bottomed playpen for a baby, who is invited to explore the room from a soft mat.
Architecture: Carlo Santi
Photography: Gabriele Basilico/Abitare

Young muscles are exercised on the jungle gym that's a ladder to the high-up perch of the bed.
Architecture: Myron Goldfiger and Norman McGrath
Photography: Norman McGrath

Places to put things away and places to keep them out receive the bulky possessions that are the essentials of teenage explorations.
Design: Joan Halprin
Photography: H. Durston Saylor

Teenagers' needs for what sociologists call group bonding are accommodated by rooms where there's plenty of space to move about without bumping into things, to lounge, to sit, and to sleep over. The carpeted platform with its easily rearranged mattresses is a recognition of the informality of young lives as the storage wall's wild painting expresses the desire for rapid movement.
Design: Larry Durham
Photography: Michael Dunne/EWA

Both children and adults use the large, open room over the garage added to the Victorian house. Charming architectural details play on the "little house" theme. The bay window, which has a lookout perch (storage underneath) for short and tall people, the lightweight furniture that clears easily away, the desk in the niche, and the convenient toilet make this a popular room for all ages.
Architecture: Shope Reno Wharton Associates
Photography: H. Durston Saylor

CHAPTER • TWELVE
SHOPPING

The most innovative products reflect the modern preoccupations with mobility, flexibility, convertibility, and variety. The result may be a chair that folds to resemble a low-relief sculpture, a sofa that unzips into a ready-made bed, or a cabinet that casts its light on the ceiling. Such objects tend to be made in urban centers where designers are pressed to devise new solutions to the growing problem of shrinking spaces which need to accommodate many different uses.

A revived interest in decoration has resulted in fresh approaches to familiar products. The choices include lamps and fittings finished in lively colors, ceramic tiles and glass blocks which may be combined in highly individual patterns, fabrics and wallpapers printed to resemble architectural ornament. In addition, there is a growing number of art galleries and showrooms which offer furniture and rugs made in limited editions, signed and numbered by their designers whose experiments with materials and forms these represent.

Patterned glass blocks build doors, skylights, windows, and screens.
Design: Federica Maragioni.
Dibianco Imports.

Beveled leaded glass panels fit doors, fanlights, windows, and tabletops.
BDG

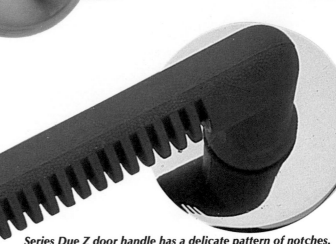

Ping Pong door and window handles also come in red, green, blue, and black.
Design: Davide Mercatali and Paolo Pedrizzetti. Domus S.p.A.

Series Due Z door handle has a delicate pattern of notches.
Design: Marco Zanuso. Valli & Colombo.

Series Otto A brass door handle fits the palm.
Design: Gae Aulenti. Valli & Colombo.

Carlton Court imitates the coffered beams of Renaissance palaces in a silk-screened ceiling paper.
Karl Mann Associates.

Soft cotton fabric is printed to look like engraved marble panels.
Design: Trix and Robert Haussmann. Mira-X.

Magic Flute is a permanently pleated polyester fabric that can become a durable window treatment.
Jack Lenor Larsen.

White wool is hand tufted to make a sculptured rug.
Design: Nob + Non. V'Soske.

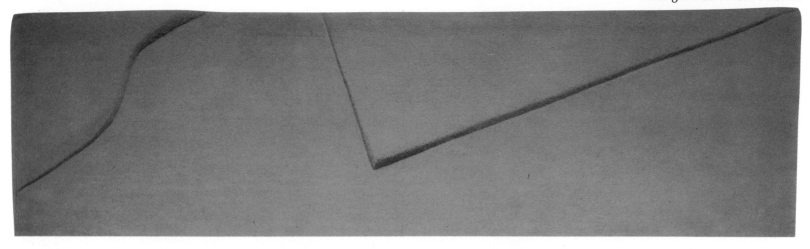

Rugged wool buffalo-plaid fabric, a popular style in apparel, has been adapted for upholstery.
Gretchen Bellinger Inc.

A striped plissé woven of silk and cotton fibers has a solid satin companion of silk and spun rayon.
Scalamandré.

Shimmering pleated silk brings couture opulence to home design.
Gretchen Bellinger Inc.

The permanently puckered texture of this cotton plissé makes for a frothy delicate fabric.
"Venezia" from Yves Gonnet Inc.

Heavy-duty cotton velvet is treated to resist stains, soil, and crushing.
Gretchen Bellinger Inc.

The stripe motif is given a fresh look in the raised and patterned weave of this cotton fabric.
Brunschwig & Fils.

Lacquered polyester fabrics add an appealing sheen to upholstered walls and furniture.
From the Ciré collection, Yves Gonnet Inc.

Silk moiré stripe is suitable for upholstery and drapery. *Brunschwig & Fils.*

A delicate cotton print is made to look like a silk taffeta lampas, which inspired its design. *Brunschwig & Fils.*

Upholstery fabric woven of cotton and viscose fibers has a glazed surface that adds shimmer to the colorful flowers. *Brunschwig & Fils.*

Solid and patterned silks are suitable for upholstery, drapery, and wall coverings. *J. Robert Scott & Associates, Inc.*

Walnut burl, Brazilian cherry, and brass are combined to add special texture to floors. *Kentucky Wood Floors Inc.*

Abstract sunset is tufted as an all-wool rug with fringe.
Design: Charles Gwathmey. V'Soske.

Fragments of color and pattern on ceramic tiles combine to make unique surfaces.
Appiani Spa/Umbrella.

Biberon table lamp has a nine-watt flourescent bulb and a metal base.
Design: Marco Zotta. Eleusi.

Suspension lamp with halogen light is made of steel and transparent sanded Perspex plate.
Design: F. D. Bartolomei. Bieffeplast.

The light is funneled upward to the hovering glass disk of the Ustorio table lamp.
Design: Alessandro de Santillana. Venini.

Sosia is a metal-shaded lamp suspended by a thin chain link.
C ing. Castaldi Illuminazione.

Hidro is a metal lamp made to light outdoor sculptures and shrubbery.
C ing. Castaldi Illuminazione.

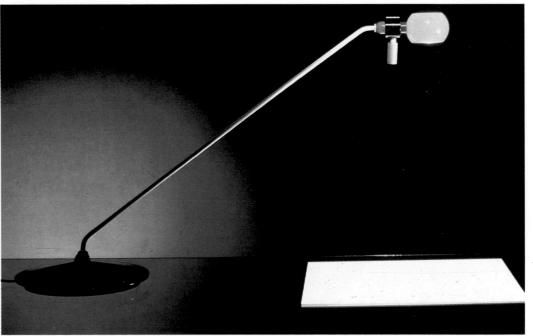

Inside the hand-blown glass shade is the Vega lamp's low-voltage, high-intensity halogen bulb.
Design: Luciano Vistosi.
Victor Lighting Corporation.

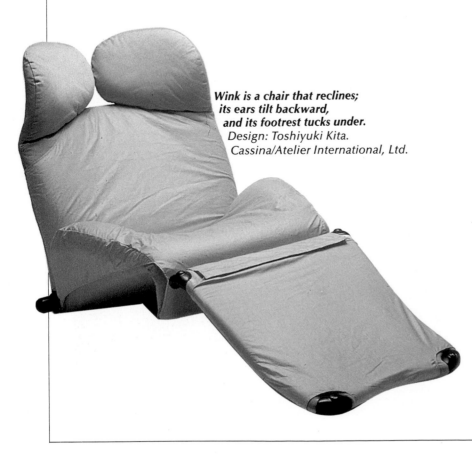

*Veranda is converted from an armchair
to a recliner by flipping up
the back and folding out the footrest.*
Design: Vico Magistretti.
Cassina/Atelier International Ltd.

*Wink is a chair that reclines;
its ears tilt backward,
and its footrest tucks under.*
Design: Toshiyuki Kita.
Cassina/Atelier International, Ltd.

*The mobile Kick table's top can be
pneumatically lowered or raised five inches.*
Design: Toshiyuki Kita. Cassina/Atelier International Ltd.

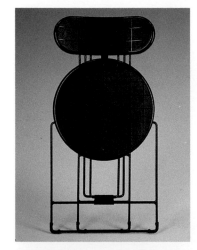

The cherry wood New Classics Armoire is seven feet tall with room for electronic equipment as well as for clothing. Design: Dakota Jackson. Dakota Jackson, Inc.

Inlaid wood is made to look like draped fabric on a mirrored cabinet. Design: Trix and Robert Haussmann. Mira-X.

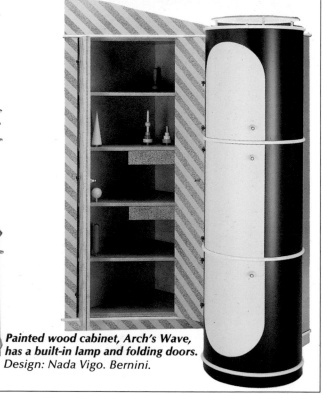

The folded Cricket chair hangs on the wall like a graphic. Design: Andries Van Onck. Magis.

Painted wood cabinet, Arch's Wave, has a built-in lamp and folding doors. Design: Nada Vigo. Bernini.

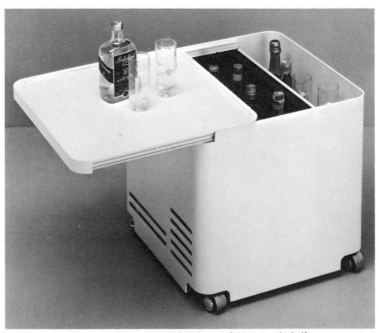

**Tubular steel, textured glass, and resilient PVC
strings create a furniture group for indoors and out.**
Design: Giandomenico Belotti. ICF Inc.

**Igloo is a refrigerator/minibar on casters
made of ABS plastic in white, black, or brown.**
Design: P. Pellegrini. Cattaneo.

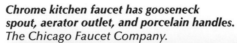

Chrome kitchen faucet has gooseneck spout, aerator outlet, and porcelain handles. *The Chicago Faucet Company.*

Sauna stool is made of birch veneer and pine. *Design: Antti Nurmesniemi. Vuokko Oy.*

Onlyou is a painted steel trolley with four circular shelves covered in textured rubber. *Design: Carlo Forcolini. Alias.*

Bright baked enamel colors renew old-fashioned fittings for kitchen and bath. *Watercolors, Inc.*

Colore Handshower may be mounted as a removable showerhead, as a hand shower, or for use as a body shower while you recline in the tub. *Watercolors, Inc.*

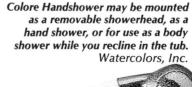

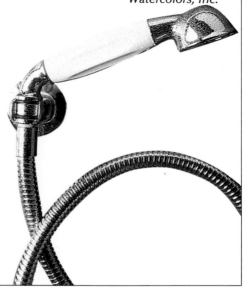

Enameled sinks come with drainers, wire basket, and chopping board. *Smeg.*

Plastic storage boxes fit under wood-sprung bed.
Biesse.

Corrugated plastic boxes with colorful storage drawers collect around cushioned modules to make sofas, chairs, and beds.
Biesse.

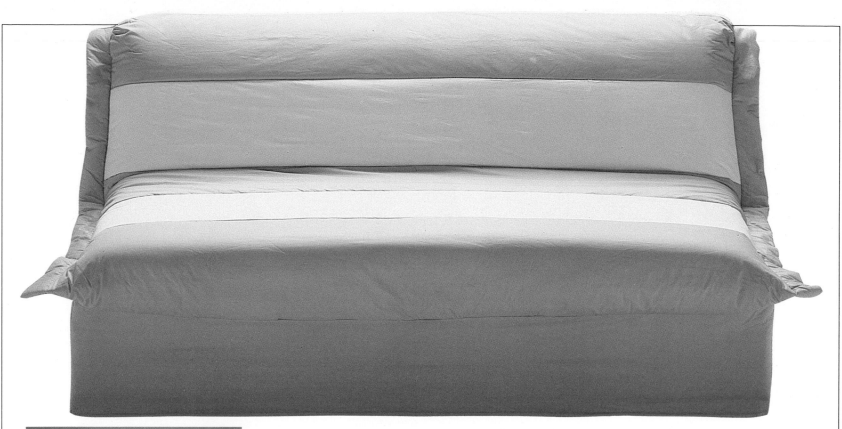

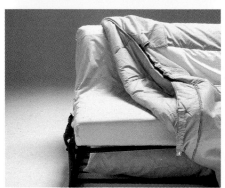

The zippered upholstery becomes the quilt as the bed unfolds and the pillows are taken out from under the frame.
Biesse.

Brightly colored legs, bases, backrest, frames, and curtains make up the many combinations of Bibi Bobo bed.
Design: Massimo Morozzi. Driade.

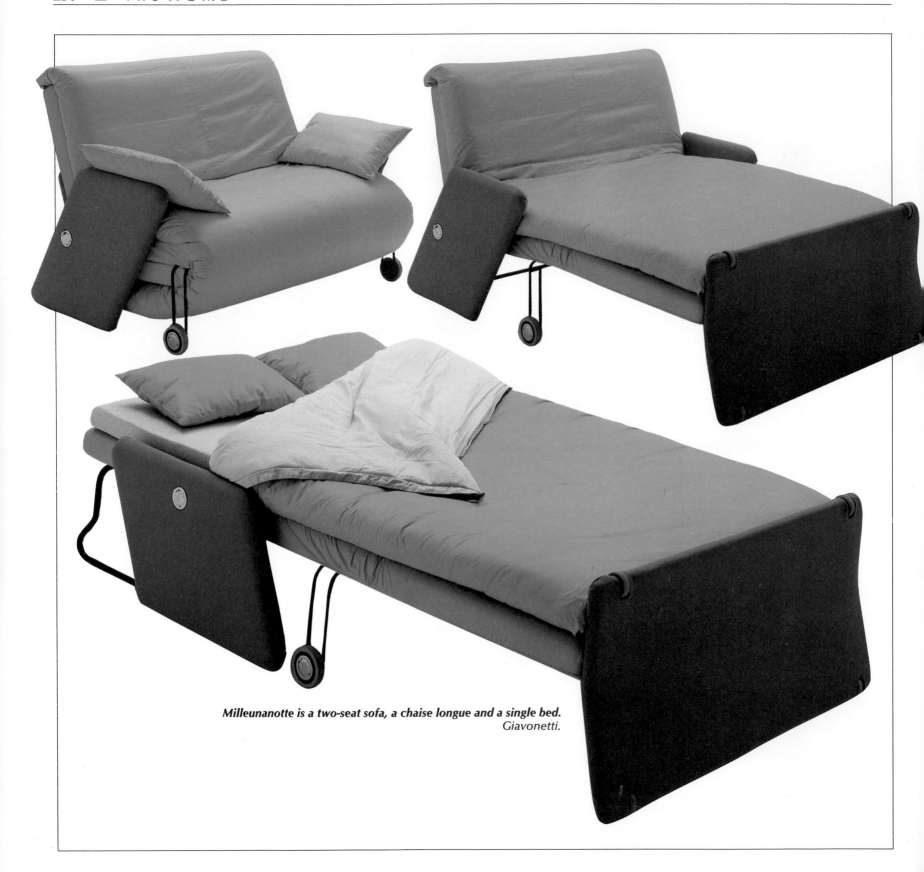

Milleunanotte is a two-seat sofa, a chaise longue and a single bed.
Giavonetti.

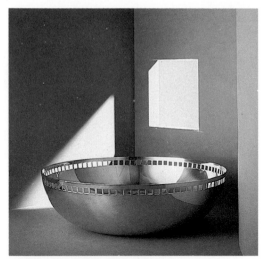

The fourteen-inch silver bowl's simple pattern enhances the austere luster of this precious metal.
Design: Richard Meier. Swid Powell Design.

This porcelain buffet plate updates the familiar colors of Florida's art deco.
Design: Laurinda Spear. Swid Powell Design.

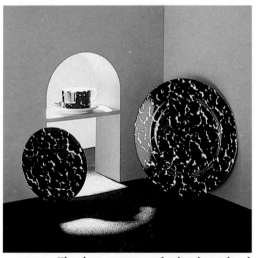

The dense pattern of school notebook covers has been adapted for buffet and dessert plates, cups and saucers.
Design: Robert Venturi. Swid Powell Design.

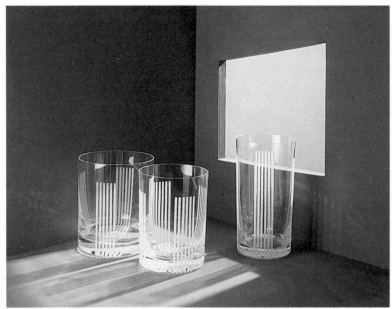

Etching on crystal barware was inspired by the Manhattan skyline.
Design: Richard Meier. Swid Powell Design.

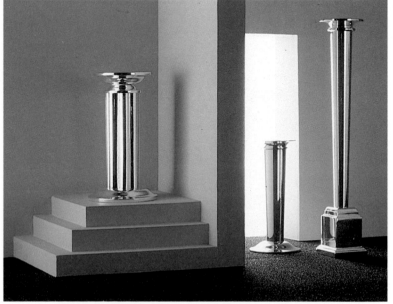

Silver candlesticks' forms are derived from the classical column.
Design: Robert A. M. Stern. Swid Powell Design.

DIBIANCO IMPORTS
8018 Third Avenue
Brooklyn, New York 11209

BDG BEVELED GLASS DESIGNS
Indianapolis Decorative
Arts Building
5420 North College Avenue
Indianapolis, Indiana 46220

DOMUS S.p.A.
25070 Lavenon (Bs) Italy
Via Case Sparse, 13
P.O. Box n. 6 Vestone

VALLI & COLOMBO
(USA) INC.
P.O. Box 245
1540 Highland Avenue
Duarte, California 91010

KARL MANN ASSOCIATES
232 East 59th Street
New York, New York 10022

MIRA-X INTERNATIONAL
FURNISHINGS, INC.
246 East Fifty-Eighth Street
New York, New York 10022

JACK LENOR LARSEN
41 East Eleventh Street
New York, New York 10003

V'SOSKE
155 East Fifty-Sixth Street
New York, New York 10022

GRETCHEN BELLINGER INC.
330 East Fifty-Ninth Street
New York, New York 10022

SCALAMANDRÉ
950 Third Avenue
New York, New York 10022

BRUNSCHWIG & FILS
75 Virginia Road
North White Plains,
New York 10603

YVES GONNET INC.
979 Third Avenue
New York, New York 10022

A P P E N D I X • O N E

PRODUCT SOURCES

(as they appear in order in Chapter Twelve)

J. ROBERT SCOTT & ASSOCIATES, INC.
8727 Melrose Avenue
Los Angeles, California 90069

APPIANI/UMBRELLA s.r.l.
Viale Felissent 48
31100 Treviso, Italy

KENTUCKY WOOD FLOORS INC.
4200 Reservoir Avenue
Louisville, Kentucky 40213

ELEUSI
via Giuseppe Verdi, 7
Casella Postale 21, Italy
22050 Lomagna (Como)

BIEFFEPLAST
P. O. Box 406
1-35100
Padova, Italy

VENINI INTERNATIONAL s.r.l.
Fondementa Vetrai 50
30121 Muraro Venezia
Italy

C ing. CASTALDI ILLUMINAZIONE
via Carlo Goldoni, 18
20090 Trezzano sul Naviglio
Milano, Italy

VICTOR LIGHTING CORPORATION
49 North East Twenty-Second Street
Miami, Florida 33137

CASSINA/ATELIER INTERNATIONAL LTD.
595 Madison Avenue
New York, New York 10022

MAGIS
31045 Motta di Livenza
Treviso, Italy

DAKOTA JACKSON, INC.
306 East Sixty-First Street
New York, New York 10021

G. B. BERNINI S.p.A.
Via Fiume 17
20048 Carate Brianza
Milano, Italy

ICF INC.
305 East Sixty-Third Street
New York, New York 10021

CATTANEO s.r.l.
22069 Rovellasca (Co), Italy
P. Za Stazione P.O. Box 25

ALIAS s.r.l.
20122 Milano, Italy
Via Respighi, 2.

SMEG ELETTRODOMETICI S.p.A.
42016 Guastalla (R.E.)
Italy

THE CHICAGO FAUCET
COMPANY
2100 South Nuclear Drive
Des Plaines, Illinois 60018

VUOKKO OY
Elimaenkatu 14
Helsinki, Finland

WATERCOLORS, INC.
Garrison-on-Hudson,
New York 10524

BIESSE S.p.A.
20035 Lissone Via Nobel 43
Italy

DRIADE S.p.A.
via Felice Casati 20
20124 Milano, Italy

GIOVANNETTI
P.O. Box 1
51032 Bottegone, Via Pierucciani
(Pistoia), Italy

SWID POWELL DESIGN
55 East Fifty-Seventh Street
New York, New York 10022

A P P E N D I X • T W O
READING

BOOKS

Arnheim, Rudolf. *The Dynamics of Architectural Form.* Berkeley, Los Angeles, London: University of California Press, 1977.

Bloomer, Kent C., and Moore, Charles W. *Body, Memory and Architecture.* New Haven and London: Yale University Press, 1977.

Gardiner, Stephen. *Evolution of the House.* Paladin, Great Britain: Granada Publishing Limited, 1976.

Giedion, Siegfried. *Mechanization Takes Command.* New York, London: W. W. Norton & Company, 1969.

Handlin, David P. *The American Home, Architecture and Society 1815-1915.* Boston, Toronto: Little, Brown and Company, 1979.

Hayden, Dolores. *Redesigning the American Dream: The Future of Housing, Work and Family Life.* New York, London: W. W. Norton and Company, 1984.

Kron, Joan. *Home-Psych: The Social Psychology of Home and Decoration.* New York: Clarkson N. Potter, Inc., 1983.

Marc, Oliver. *Psychology of the House.* London: Thames and Hudson, Ltd., 1977.

Moore, Charles; Allen, Gerald; and Lyndon, Donlyn. *The Place of Houses.* New York, Chicago, San Francisco: Holt, Rinehart and Winston, 1974.

Wharton, Edith, and Codman, Ogden, Jr. *The Decoration of Houses.* New York: W. W. Norton & Company, Inc., 1978.

Wright, David, and Andrejko, Dennis. *Passive Solar Architecture, Logic and Beauty.* New York, Cincinnati, Toronto, London, Melbourne: Van Nostrand Reinhold, 1982.

Wright, Frank Lloyd. *The Natural House.* New York and Scarborough, Ontario: A Meridan Book, New American Library, Times Mirror, 1970.

Wright, Gwendolyn. *Building the Dream: A Social History of Housing in America.* New York: Pantheon Books, 1981.

PERIODICALS

Abitare

Architectural Digest

Architectural Record Houses

Domus

House and Garden

House Beautiful

Industrial Design

Interior Design

Progressive Architecture

The New York Times

INDEX